Wicked
MUNCIE

Wicked MUNCIE

KEITH ROYSDON AND
DOUGLAS WALKER

THE
History
PRESS

Published by The History Press
Charleston, SC
www.historypress.net

First published 2016

Manufactured in the United States

ISBN 978.1.46713.665.5

Library of Congress Control Number: 2016941429

CONTENTS

INTRODUCTION

More than a few midwestern cities claimed the nickname "Little Chicago" and all that implied: crime, corruption and, at times, a swaggering boastfulness about that reputation.

But Muncie, Indiana, was one of the few towns that truly earned the title.

Since its founding in the late 1820s, Muncie—a little less than an hour northeast of Indianapolis by modern travel methods—has been a city of contradictions. Thousands of people came to Muncie from the south and east, hoping to make their fortunes, or at least a decent living, in the city's twentieth-century factories. They worked hard and turned the city into a manufacturing powerhouse until the dawn of the twenty-first century, when most of the surviving factories closed.

But many came here for the city's reputation as a town open to risk-taking and lawbreaking. Gambling, prostitution and liquor—and the people who provided those vices—ruled the less-genteel neighborhoods of Muncie. Occasionally, a crusading newspaper publisher, daredevil cop or by-the-book prosecuting attorney called out lawbreakers or even tried to curb them.

Along with the risk-takers came the harsher elements of society: the thieves and con artists and murderers. Sometimes they were easily recognized by their deeds, and sometimes they were even caught in the act. Sometimes the influential and supposedly respectable turned their hands against their neighbors, believing they were above the law.

Too often, they were right.

Since the early 1900s, Muncie has been considered the typical small American city, thanks to the famous "Middletown" sociological study. The city has a firm place in pop culture. Talk show host David Letterman graduated from college here, *Garfield* creator Jim Davis drew his comic here and movies like *Close Encounters of the Third Kind* and TV shows like *The X-Files* set stories here. The list of pop culture references to Muncie is long and amusing.

But Muncie has been anything but typical in the grim and oddball incidents that have marked its history. From public officials who spent time in jail to mysterious murders, from unfortunate encounters that ended in mayhem to offbeat crimes, from notorious madams who ran for public office to a gypsy king buried here, Muncie has long been in the headlines.

As these stories unfolded, some publicity-conscious Muncie officials have had an inclination to suppress what they viewed as "negative" news. In decades past, however, that mania for secrecy—and willingness to hide the truth—at times reached such a level that decisions were seemingly made to let murders go unsolved and killers go unpunished.

By recounting these stories from the 1890s to the 1970s, *Wicked Muncie* gives readers a look at the city that many have heard of but few know. Some of the stories are amusing. Some are dark. Some are astounding. Some are heartbreaking.

To read these stories is to know the city: its dim taverns, its dank jail cells and its bright courtrooms, where justice was—sometimes—served.

1

"A WIDE-OPEN TOWN"

The shootout at Muncie's New Deal Cigar Store—at 1:20 a.m. on Thursday, October 13, 1949—left two men dead, a third mortally wounded and four others nursing gunshot wounds.

The bullets fired that morning in the 600 block of South Walnut Street, just north of the tracks, also inflicted grievous wounds on Muncie's image, creating ripples that would damage local reputations and careers.

A resulting eighteen-day murder trial of two southern Indiana men, accused of coming to Muncie to rob participants in a poker game at the New Deal, "hung the city's dirty linen on a public clothesline daily," a local newspaper suggested.

"I blame Muncie politicians for the deaths of [the] men in the gambling den," Reverend John C. Roberts of the Muncie Ministerial Association told reporters a day after the shootings. "Politicians have let gambling and boozing run wide open in Muncie. They have the blood of these men on their hands. …Muncie is the Midwest Mecca for fugitives from the law."

In the end, local authorities, stinging from widespread criticism, appeared to lose interest in pursuing justice in the New Deal case. An event that sent three men to their graves would result in a single defendant serving five years in prison.

There would be conflicting narratives concerning what exactly unfolded in the cigar store that night before the bullets began to fly.

Bedford residents Donald Franklin Dalton, twenty-six, and George Edward Gratzer, twenty-seven, said they came to Muncie on October 12 looking

Corner Where Fatal Shots Were Fired

The Muncie Star Photo by Bob Brown

One of the two gunmen who slew two and wounded four in an abortive hold-up at the New Deal Cigar Store, 664 South Walnut street, early yesterday morning, opened his barrage of fire from this spot at the rear of the gambling room of the New Deal. He was seated next to the washstand in one of these three chairs when the alarm was sounded and the firing began. When this picture was taken shortly after the incident, blood from one of the slain still covered the linoleum at lower left.

The bloodstained back room of the New Deal Cigar Store on South Walnut Street in Muncie, where three men were fatally shot on October 13, 1949. *Courtesy of the* Muncie Star.

for a card game. Finding one, evidence suggests, likely wasn't much of a challenge.

Prosecutors would contend that the out-of-towners walked into the New Deal intending to commit armed robbery.

The manager of the cigar store, Ralph Frazier, told police that about ten men were playing poker when he noticed a stranger—later identified as Gratzer—standing near the table.

At that point, he said, another man—later identified as Dalton—entered the shop with a gun and announced, "Just don't do anything and nobody will get hurt. This is a stickup."

Frazier said he shouted, "Look out, boys, he's got a gun!"

"A burst of gunfire followed," the Associated Press reported. Some estimated as many as a dozen shots were fired.

One of the bullets hit Frazier, forty, in the torso, passing through his liver and right lung. He would die of his wounds about fifty hours later in Ball Memorial Hospital.

A poker player, Dewey Wills, described as a fifty-four-year-old factory worker, was shot several times in the abdomen. He staggered to the shop's front door, where he fell dead.

Another participant in the card game, Theodore Rains, forty-three—a Muncie restaurant owner and father of five daughters—was shot in the heart. His body was found under the poker table.

Three other cigar store patrons suffered less severe wounds. In an era before medical privacy laws, photographs of the victims in their hospital beds—even the dying Frazier—were published in the city's newspapers.

And Muncie police soon found yet another victim of the shootout.

Alleged bandit Gratzer—believed to have been shot in the stomach, accidentally, by Dalton—was found in Dalton's Buick sedan near Heekin Park, at Grant Street and Memorial Drive.

Dalton, however, was nowhere to be found.

Taken to the hospital, Gratzer was rushed into surgery and then was interviewed by the Muncie Police Department's lead detective, Merv Collins. (Also that morning, Dalton's wife, Anna Mae, gave birth to their son in a Bedford hospital.)

While Gratzer later denied making most of the statements attributed to him by Collins, he purportedly said that Dalton had fatally shot Wills and Rains while he shot Frazier by accident during a struggle.

Newspaper coverage included photos taken at the shooting scene, some showing blood on the floor of the cigar store and a bullet hole in a wall, only inches from a framed photograph of Indiana governor Henry Schricker.

(Signs on the wall prohibited gamblers from drinking at the card tables and from asking to borrow money. Another read, "All cards must be cut.")

In the wake of the shootings, Pastor Roberts of the Muncie Ministerial Association told the International News Service that he would urge Governor Schricker to station state troopers in Muncie until the city's "open gambling" could be brought under control.

Reached by the *Evening Press* via "long-distance telephone," the governor said he would help local authorities in all ways possible, but he did not commit to putting Muncie under the control of state police.

Mayor Lester Holloway expressed frustration over allegations of corruption aimed at Muncie in the wake of the New Deal Cigar Store slayings. *Courtesy of Muncie Newspapers, Inc.*

"I want to put down murder and catch murderers as much as anyone else," the governor said.

The next week saw a grand jury investigation of the shootings begin.

The ministerial association sent the grand jurors a message—signed by local pastors Russell Hiatt and Robert Morris—urging the panel to "use your power to compel enforcement of the laws against gambling and other forms of vice."

Muncie, the pastors wrote, was "notorious as a haven for gamblers, prostitutes and criminals."

"The FBI reports that Muncie has one of the highest crime rates in the nation," they added. "Medical reports show that Muncie ranks high in the prevalence of venereal diseases."

Mayor Lester Holloway bristled at the growing criticism of law enforcement and of widespread gambling in his city.

"How are you going to stop that?" he asked. "You can't change people. You can't just appoint a guardian over them to go along with them to keep them from doing it."

The Democratic mayor said he believed he and the city were being unfairly condemned, saying the shootings could have taken place "in Anderson, or any other community in Indiana, or Ohio."

"I don't care what happens in Muncie, you stub your toe and you don't like me, you will put the blame on me for it," Holloway said. "I guess that's part of the job."

The mayor said he didn't intend to discuss the case further.

"I'm not going to be a party to keeping that kind of publicity going," he said.

Police chief Harry Nelson said the blame for the slayings rested solely with Gratzer and Dalton, a pair of "trigger-happy punks."

Delaware County sheriff W. "Pete" Anthony, meanwhile, said the county council was not giving him enough resources to combat gambling.

"I most certainly think the members of the county council do not want the law enforced," he said. "If they did, they'd give me more help."

Anthony added that if council members "want the law enforced and gambling closed up…they'll give me a vice squad of three men."

On October 18, the grand jury indicted Gratzer, recovering from his bullet wound, and Dalton, still at large, on first-degree murder charges. The panel also issued a statement finding law enforcement lax in Delaware County.

Thirteen days after the shootings, Don Dalton was captured in San Antonio, Texas.

A reporter there described Dalton as "a self-styled gambler who outfitted himself like a cowboy when he hit Texas."

"The papers said it was a holdup, but it wasn't that way at all," Dalton said of the events in Muncie. "It was self-defense."

He maintained he had been playing poker at the New Deal that night, and winning, before he was angrily accused of cheating.

Dalton said he had been shot in the left hand while trying to gather his winnings. Then someone turned the lights out in the cigar store, prompting several of the card players—including Dalton—to produce guns and fire into the darkness, he said.

"There were about thirty men grabbing at me," Dalton claimed.

Dalton would give somewhat different accounts of the night in question when he and Gratzer's Delaware Circuit Court trial began in late February 1950.

Dalton Takes Stand in Own Defense

The Muncie Star Photo

Don Dalton, left, on Friday, took the witness stand in his own defense. Court Reporter Margaret Garrison takes the testimony while Judge Joseph H. Davis presides over the trial in Circuit Court.

Donald Dalton testifies at his 1950 trial on three murder charges, stemming from a 1949 shootout at Muncie's New Deal Cigar Store. *Courtesy of the* Muncie Star.

Attorney Ed Lewis of Indianapolis, defending Dalton, proved accurate in a prediction made in his opening remarks to jurors.

"We're going to put the city of Muncie on trial," he promised.

Another defense attorney, Clarence Benadum of Muncie, assured the jury that "a gambling house is a long way from a pink tea." He went so far as to compare Muncie's gambling joints to the "slime pits of the Vale of Siddim" referred to in the Old Testament.

An attorney for Gratzer, Robert Mellen, noted Muncie's reputation for gambling and vice.

"Muncie has police who cannot see and will not act," he said.

Another of Gratzer's lawyers, Van Ogle, like Benadum was a former Delaware County prosecutor. He took aim at Mayor Holloway.

"I say to you I've never seen the town as open as it is now," Ogle said. "I am going to drag it out of the alleys and set it on the front doorstep of the mayor. He's the man who runs your town."

On the witness stand, police detective Collins said that, while being interrogated a few hours after the shootings, a wounded Gratzer told him he and Dalton came to Muncie "looking around for a place to knock off."

Grilled by defense attorney Lewis about the seemingly open gambling operations at the New Deal and in other Muncie establishments, Collins said, "All the years I have been on the department, I don't remember ever receiving a call, not one, [about] the New Deal Cigar Store."

The block of South Walnut Street where the New Deal was located had been referred to by a defense attorney as Muncie's "Barbary Coast," a reference to a notorious waterfront district in San Francisco.

Collins disagreed. "Some of the best businessmen in Muncie are located in that section," he said.

Gratzer—wearing a button reflecting his military service in World War II—discounted any statements he made to Collins that reflected he and Dalton had been planning a robbery.

He said he was under the influence of morphine when questioned by the police detective.

Dalton, for his part, during the trial issued a statement through his attorneys indicating that he and Gratzer had been threatened—for reasons they didn't understand—by the men in the cigar store and that he ran to his car and retrieved his gun in an effort to rescue Gratzer from their attackers.

On the witness stand, Dalton recanted a statement he had given to FBI agents after his arrest in Texas, even though it carried his signature.

He said he had signed the document without reading it.

"I have a great deal of faith in the federal government," Dalton told the jury. "I didn't think they would put anything in the statement I didn't say."

The trial drew huge, sometimes raucous, crowds to the third-floor courtroom.

"There were cheers as Dalton described '25 or 30' gambling places here," the *Evening Press* reported.

Judge Joseph Davis at times rebuked the spectators for their outbursts.

"This is your court, and you are welcome," he said. "But there must not be any show of emotion. No applause. No cheering."

According to newspaper accounts, women ate sandwiches in the courtroom, not wanting to surrender their coveted seats during lunch breaks. A man wanting to keep his seat fought off hunger by eating a large number of bananas.

A local radio station broadcast the Dalton-Gratzer trial, with microphones set up at the defense and prosecution tables, the witness stand and the judge's bench.

Sheriff Anthony said at least six spectators fainted during the trial, and an elderly spectator suffered a heart attack.

Cleo Mann, operator of a concession stand in the courthouse, reported that on the Friday when attorneys made their final arguments, he sold eighteen cases of soft drinks, more than 150 buns and about eighty pies.

In his closing remarks, the always-colorful Benadum told the jury, "The gambling house where Wild Bill Hickok was shot compared very favorably to the New Deal Cigar Store. ...It's a long way from a Sunday school class."

Defense attorney Lewis suggested police had intimidated witnesses in the case.

"As long as your good city of Muncie continues to have slime pits in its midst like that New Deal Cigar Store, you will have killings," he added.

The Indianapolis lawyer then paid tribute to the "fine people" of Muncie and Delaware County and to the county prosecutor, Guy Ogle, brother of defense attorney Van Ogle.

Lewis said he would be willing to socialize with the prosecutor anywhere in the city, "except the New Deal Cigar Store."

That prompted loud laughter in the gallery.

Deputy prosecutor Frank Massey called Dalton and Gratzer "gamblers and cheats."

"They were pretty well armed for two boys just looking around for a place to play poker," he said, adding that defense lawyers had tried to "clutter up this court with red herrings."

Defense lawyer Van Ogle said the only "smoke screen" in the case was at the New Deal Cigar Store.

"They've got eighteen feet of cigar store and forty feet of gambling room, and they've put up a screen up so you can't see," he said, drawing more laughs.

Aware of the statements in closing arguments that blistered the local police department, detective Collins at one point called court staff and asked, "Have they still got me on trial up there?"

After a full night of deliberations, Judge Davis sent the jury to the Delaware Hotel for what proved to be about five hours of sleep.

After about twenty-two total hours of deliberating, the jury indicated it was hopelessly deadlocked. Davis told it to keep working.

A few hours later, the verdicts were in.

Don Dalton was found guilty of murder, and the jury recommended he receive a life sentence.

"Oh, Don! Oh, Don!" his wife cried, putting her head on the defense table and weeping.

George Gratzer, however, was found not guilty. In the wake of the verdicts, he stood next to his wife, appearing "pleased and at the same time stunned," the *Evening Press* reported.

After the trial, Dalton told the *Press* he was glad his co-defendant would be able to go home to Bedford.

"I came to Muncie to gamble because I heard it was a wide-open town," Dalton said. "Then I ran into a hornet's nest, and I did the best I could to get out."

Benadum said Dalton was being made "a scapegoat," calling his client's conviction "a cowardly, half-hearted gesture to condemn organized gambling in this city."

Dalton's wheelchair-bound mother, Elizabeth, had testified at the trial about how much anguish her son's gambling activities caused her.

"I would rather follow my boy to his grave, even yet today, than to see him go into a gambling place," she said.

After the verdict was announced, Mrs. Dalton made a public appeal for donations to help fund an appeal of her son's conviction.

"I spent every dime I have for this trial," the mother said. "I mortgaged my home for a lot of the money we needed."

Her son's case, however, was anything but over.

Four months later, Judge Davis granted Dalton's motion for a new trial on the grounds that evidence that he had killed the three victims was "not conclusive."

That trial—which likely would have resulted in still more statewide publicity about Muncie's perceived evils—was planned for November 1950.

That October 17, however, in what seemed to be a hastily scheduled hearing, Dalton pleaded guilty to a reduced count of manslaughter and was promptly sentenced to two to twenty-one years in prison.

Prosecutor Guy Ogle expressed frustration, saying he did not have legal grounds to contest Dalton's plea to the lesser charge, although newspaper articles from the time and court records do not reflect why he could not have continued to pursue the murder charges.

A few weeks after the abrupt end of the New Deal case, Merv Collins resigned from his job as chief of detectives, citing health reasons.

The veteran lawman—who helped capture notorious gangster Gerald Chapman in 1925 and nearly arrested John Dillinger in 1933—had not yet reached his fifty-third birthday when he died in March 1952.

Lester Holloway's bid for a second term as Muncie mayor ended in the 1951 Democratic primary, when he was soundly defeated by Mario Pieroni, a local attorney who happened to be blind.

That November, Republican Joe Barclay defeated Pieroni—who later served as a Delaware County judge—in the mayoral election.

Republicans also won seven of nine Muncie City Council races that year. (Democrats had won a seven-to-two council majority four years earlier.)

Don Dalton's name was back in the headlines in April 1954, when he walked away from an inmate work crew at the Morgan-Monroe State Forest.

He remained at large until early June, when he called authorities and said his sister would deliver him to the Indiana Reformatory in Pendleton later that day.

The Indiana Parole Board apparently didn't hold Dalton's weeks on the lam against him.

On October 8, 1955—a week short of five years after his arrival at the reformatory—Dalton was granted parole and set free.

George Gratzer was sixty-five, still living in Bedford and still married to Anna Mae, when he died in July 1988.

Don Dalton lived to the age of eighty-one, passing away in Big River, California, in April 2004.

His obituary reflected Dalton had owned a carpet-cleaning business in Phoenix, Arizona, for forty years.

"He enjoyed playing poker at his favorite casino," it added.

THE FUNERAL OF THE GYPSY KING

Some called Muncie home. Some were just passing through—often with a police escort to hurry them on their way.

They were very seldom welcome.

They were gypsies.

During much of the twentieth century, the Romani people who lived in Muncie and sometimes just traveled through were considered amusing diversions at best and criminals at worst. The derogatory name commonly applied to them was a label and description wrapped up in one unpleasant package.

In the mid-twentieth century, the gypsies were the go-to suspects when Muncie police investigated complaints of theft or fraud. Muncie police set up sting operations to bust local palm readers and fortunetellers.

But for three days in 1956, Muncie mourned, along with the members of his tribe, the death of a gypsy king.

The Romani people, hailing from Europe and Russia, began arriving in the United States in the 1880s. They were known as gypsies in part because their roots were believed to be in Egypt.

Evansville, in the far southern corner of Indiana, is the site of the grave of Elizabeth Harrison, considered by many to be a "gypsy queen." Harrison died in 1895 but wasn't buried until six months later, when word of her passing brought dozens of gypsies and thousands of onlookers for her funeral services.

As their people weaved their way through the tapestry of the United States, it's not surprising that Muncie—at the crossroads of America—

The tombstone of Miller Thompson in Beech Grove Cemetery. *Courtesy of Keith Roysdon.*

became a destination or, at least, a brief stop along the way to somewhere else for many Romani.

In the 1950s, the salting of Muncie's population with the traveling tradesmen known as gypsies made for an uneasy mix. Muncie's population was made up, to a great extent, of not only native-born Hoosiers but also thousands of people from the southern United States who came to work in the city's many manufacturing plants.

By the midcentury, the city had shrugged off the control of the Ku Klux Klan, but there was little tolerance for society's outliers.

So when Muncie residents began complaining about an automobile fender repair scam in the spring of 1952, fingers were quickly pointed toward gypsies.

Herman Cumings told police he had entrusted the repair of dents in his car to a couple of men he later identified as gypsies. Armed with ball peen hammers, the men banged around on the car for a while and then told Cumings they really needed to take his car to a garage to work on it.

When they brought the car back, Cumings's fender was miraculously smooth. The men warned him not to touch it because he would mar the paint job. After he paid thirty-three dollars for the work, however, Cumings couldn't resist. He poked the fender, and his finger sank into what was described in the *Muncie Star* as "furnace cement." Other parts of the car had more dents than when the gypsies took it away for repairs, Cumings said.

Another Muncie man, Omar Tull, said he was "manhandled" by two men who "appeared to be gypsies" after he refused to let them fix a dent in his fender.

After that report, police journeyed just south of Muncie, where a gypsy camp was set up along Indiana 3, a state highway. Cops told the leaders of the camp to keep their people in line.

Whether gypsies were really to blame for a rash of such crimes in the years to follow is hard to say. Newspaper accounts report the matter-of-fact blaming of gypsies.

Muncie's relationship with the travelers got worse and odder.

In the summer of 1952, seventy-nine-year-old Eli Cross told police that he had been advised that his rheumatism could be cured at a special church service east of the city. The advice came from men he described as "gypsies."

After the men left, Cross discovered his pocket had been picked of forty-five dollars.

And as it turned out, there was no special service featuring miracle cures at the specified church.

A Muncie woman complained to police that several gypsies tried to force her to…sell some of her chickens. That account came from the woman's husband.

"Tell 'em to stay out of here," was the word put forth by Muncie police captain Jack Ertel in the late summer of 1952. Police sent word to the gypsy camp south of the city that Muncie was "off limits."

Newspapers joking referred to Muncie's "unofficial immigration office," noting that police chief E.O. Rust had "deported" two men spotted "acting in a manner indicating they were up to no good."

Exactly what those actions were was not explained.

Rust "deported the two from Muncie after a stern warning that their next visit here would find any and all of the gypsy band so far back in the jail cells that they'll lose their summer tan."

Through the rest of the 1950s and into the 1960s, gypsies made the news for offering cut-rate auto repairs, stealing clothing and food and promising cures for rheumatism.

In one case in the summer of 1961, "fast-talking gypsies" promised a man a cure for rheumatism, grabbing the man and shaking his legs and pants. After the men left, their victim discovered they had somehow gotten into his wallet and removed twelve dollars.

By the late 1950s, local police had taken to "escorting" gypsy caravans from one county line to another to make sure they didn't stop in Muncie. One summer night, Deputy Sheriff Delbert Knight heard that gypsies had left Fort Wayne and were headed for Muncie.

Knight met the caravan, including fifteen house trailers and several pickup trucks, north of the city and escorted them across the county line to the south.

There were moments when Muncie residents seemed interested or even amused by the Romani people who lived in the city. Just before Christmas 1960, a gypsy holiday celebration attended by prominent attorney Clarence Benadum was covered by the *Muncie Star*.

A photo shows Benadum receiving a "gypsy good luck coin" from one of the women of the Eli family at the party. But that holiday feeling didn't last.

In the spring of 1963, Muncie fortuneteller Rita Eli was arrested and charged in a police investigation into complaints that she "did unlawfully pretend, for money, to predict future events."

In a "sting" operation, Muncie police sent a female officer to a rented building along South Walnut Street, where the Eli women were telling fortunes, contrary to local ordinances.

The wheels of justice didn't move quickly against the Elis, however. Two years later, trials for Rita and Ruby Eli on charges of fortunetelling had been postponed six times. Attorney Benadum, representing the Elis, moved for a further postponement because the trial would coincide with Greek Orthodox holidays. A judge granted the request.

"In a magnanimous gesture of appreciation, the defendants, through Benadum, invited the court to partake of the whole, barbecued lamb waiting patiently at their home," according to one newspaper account.

> Benadum described the feast of whole, barbecued lamb, seasoned with oregano, garlic and other spices and laid out on a table with an icon and candles commemorating the feat of St. George. He said the gypsies invite as many as possible in the belief the more people in attendance, the greater the blessings, hence the invitation to the court, prosecution and witnesses.

A few days later, Ruby Eli was found guilty of fortunetelling and fined forty-five dollars. There was no word on how the lamb turned out.

Tensions between Muncie police and gypsies continued into the 1980s, when newspaper accounts of "dark-complected" women "described as looking like gypsies" were sought for the theft of thousands of dollars from store cash registers and safes. When police couldn't find the specific women in "brightly colored dresses" in one incident, a group of travelers believed to be gypsies were escorted to the county line.

Sometimes the attitude toward gypsies was softened. One Indiana expert noted that gypsy lore pointing to them as thieves also included a hugely mitigating factor. Just before the crucifixion, a gypsy stole one of the four nails that were to be hammered into Jesus Christ. Because Christ was spared some pain, according to the myth, God gave the gypsies the right to steal.

One notable moment when Muncie felt charitable, even a kind of kinship, toward gypsies came in June 1956, when a gypsy tribe elder died in the town.

Miller Thompson was sixty-six years old when he died in Muncie. The coppersmith was born to Brazilian parents in Zuni, Virginia, but somehow ended up in Muncie. He had been sick with an illness unspecified in newspaper accounts when he died in a hospital near the Midway gypsy camp south of the town.

Identified in the newspaper as "the former leader of a tribe of roving tradesmen"—the article nowhere uses the word "gypsy"—Thompson's life was first celebrated by a "ceremonial feast" at the camp.

Several feasts were held over the course of three days following his death and drew crowds of Muncie onlookers.

Beech Grove Cemetery. *Courtesy of Ball State University archives.*

"At least 200" relatives and friends of Thompson gathered for his funeral service at Meeks Mortuary in Muncie.

As Thompson's son, Ephraim, led "mournful chanting," floral arrangements were placed around the casket. More than two thousand red and white carnations were used.

Community leaders—unnamed in newspaper accounts—visited the mortuary to pay their respects. They marveled over not only the crowd and flowers but also a brazier in which incense burned and "two huge candelabra."

Thompson's funeral procession stopped Muncie traffic and prompted gapes from onlookers. Cars in the funeral procession carried license plates from Arizona, New York, Missouri and other states.

The gypsy leader's final journey was completed on the shoulders of his comrades, who bore the casket not only into the mortuary but also into city-owned Beech Grove Cemetery.

Although Muncie was suspicious of gypsies for most of the first half of the twentieth century, the city was respectful of and fascinated by the death of a gypsy king.

A Child Stands Trial for Murder

No crime, perhaps, is more disturbing to a community than the killing of a child. A Muncie case that unfolded as the nineteenth century came to an end had that and more: a defendant, on trial for murder as an adult, who was twelve years old when the crime took place.

Five-year-old Antonio "Andy" Bodenmiller became the target of a massive search in Whitely—then described as a northeast-side "suburb"—when he failed to return home for dinner on Monday, November 14, 1898.

A local newspaper that week reported that Andy—also known to friends as "Boomer"—had "habits and character as pure as the snow…and wore golden locks of curls that played about his neck and shoulders with gave him a feminine air that was decidedly attractive."

The overnight search—largely focused on the "Whitely woods," part of what is now McCulloch Park—was fruitless.

About noon the following day, however, local barber William Warrenger was walking past an abandoned sand pit several yards west of Broadway when an overturned container in the sand and gravel caught his eye.

As he approached, the horrified barber saw "a tiny hand protruding from (under) the box."

He alerted police, who turned the box over and made the grisly confirmation that it held the remains of the missing child.

The boy's body had obviously been forced into the lidless box, and the child's appearance prompted speculation that he had been the victim of a fatal beating.

This *Muncie Daily Herald* sketch of slaying victim Antonio "Andy" Miller is based on a photo taken when the boy was three, two years before his shooting death. *Courtesy of the* Muncie Daily Herald.

Freddie Oland was thirteen when he was tried as an adult in the 1898 slaying of five-year-old Antonia "Andy" Miller. *Courtesy of the* Muncie Daily Herald.

A hole dug in the sand near the box led investigators to believe an effort to bury the boy's body had been abandoned, perhaps when searchers approached in the darkness the previous night.

An autopsy would reveal Andy had been shot, near the right temple, with the .32-caliber bullet traveling down through his brain and striking the top of his spinal column, "causing instant death." Powder burns indicated the shot had been fired at close range.

The search for the missing child quickly became a manhunt for an unknown killer.

The *Muncie Morning News* directed its attention to the Bodenmiller household, on the east side of Broadway, not far from the sand pit.

"The fact that the child's parents had his life insured, and the claim that the father is addicted to drink and has had serious family altercations has led to some expressions that the crime was committed with the knowledge of the parents," the *News* reported the day after the body was discovered.

Such speculation would end quickly. On November 16, police investigators—and former Muncie mayor Charles Kilgore—were canvassing the area for clues when a boy about Andy's age told them he and his older brother had witnessed the shooting.

Mikey Betts identified the assailant as twelve-year-old Frederick Horace "Freddie" Oland, saying he had gunned down Andy after the little boy threw a stone in his direction as the youngsters stood near the sand pit.

Oland's father owned a saloon along Broadway. The Olands lived in the same building, as did his accuser's family and other tenants.

That afternoon, Freddie Oland was playing his guitar at home when police asked him to accompany them to the nearby Whitely Hotel for questioning. A news account would report that a Captain Turner "took Oland in a private room on his lap and began questioning."

"I wanted to talk to him as if he were my own child, and told him to tell the truth," Turner would later testify.

"Fred, there is no use of you lying any further," ex-Mayor Kilgore told the suspect. "We have good Christian women who saw you do this, and if you say it, you will be all right, as it was accidental."

The youth agreed to give a statement if his mother was present.

When she arrived, Freddie said, "Mama, I did it. I killed poor Andy. But it happened when I was shooting at a rabbit."

"Oh, my God!" his mother cried.

Oland described firing a shot from some distance away with a rifle. He said the mortally wounded victim had toppled into a box he was standing next to, which then overturned into the pit.

A few minutes later, he recanted. Freddie Oland from that point on maintained that he knew nothing about the slaying of Andy Bodenmiller.

That night, a crowd gathered outside the hotel. There were suggestions of mob violence and apparently threats to lynch Samuel Jackson, a black employee at Orland's father's nearby saloon.

Freddie Oland, despite his age, was taken to the Delaware County jail.

The next day, the *Morning News* described the suspect as "a mean boy, always ready to fight with a knife or revolver."

It recounted an earlier incident that saw Oland and other neighborhood boys wrap a rope around Andy's neck and then "string him up" until he was "almost dead, with his tongue hanging out."

(A later clarification acknowledged the newspaper was uncertain which boys had been involved in the near-hanging.)

Police seized guns from the Oland tavern and home. None, it turned out, was a .32-caliber weapon.

That week, Andy Bodenmiller's funeral was held at St. Lawrence Catholic Church. It was reported to have drawn the largest crowd for a child's funeral in city history.

On November 25, the still-incarcerated Freddie Oland testified for an hour before a Delaware County grand jury. Four days later, he was indicted on a murder charge.

On December 1, a judge allowed Oland's father to post a $2,000 bond to secure his son's release.

By the time he stood trial in April 1899, Freddie was thirteen. He was reported to be "bowing to acquaintances and chatting with his father and mother" as he showed up for the first day of proceedings.

On the witness stand, Freddie again insisted that he knew nothing about the child's killing and maintained he and the victim had been "very friendly."

He and his mother testified he was in downtown Muncie, running errands for his parents and playing pool, when Andy went missing.

His chief accuser's mother, meanwhile, insisted her young son had been seriously ill on the day Andy was killed and never went outside.

An insurance investigator said he had collected soil samples, possibly with traces of blood, at the gravel pit, giving them to Mayor Edward Tuhey for sake-keeping.

Mayor Tuhey testified that the envelopes containing the soil had disappeared from his office.

Classmates testified that the defendant was one of several students at the Whitely school who routinely carried a handgun.

Freddie Oland's attorneys suggested John Petty, "a fresh-faced man of about thirty," was a more likely suspect than their client.

Petty had operated a painting business in Whitely, which he abruptly closed about six weeks after the slaying, moving to Ohio. He testified that before leaving town, he had painted the floor of his business, not to hide bloodstains, but because it was "spotted up with paint and tobacco spittle."

The jury was given the case on the late afternoon of April 20. Jurors went out to supper, then came back to the courthouse and quickly returned a not-guilty verdict.

"I knew it would be that way," the young defendant told reporters, also thanking the local media for its "kindness and fairness."

As jurors lined up to shake hands with the acquitted teenager, one told him, "Now Fred, never carry firearms again."

Entrance to Beech Grove Cemetery, Muncie, Ind.

After he was shot to death in what is now McCulloch Park in 1898, young Andy Miller was buried in Beech Grove Cemetery. Surviving records don't reflect the location of his grave, however. *Courtesy of Ball State University archives.*

A few days before Christmas 1923, a bandit followed Fred Oland, then thirty-seven, from the downtown theater he managed to his home on East Wysor Street. As he got out of his car, the man pulled a gun and demanded money.

Oland produced his own handgun, which malfunctioned after firing a single bullet. The bandit also fired once, sending a bullet through the theater manager's hand. By the time it passed through his heavy winter coat, however, it had slowed to the degree that it glanced off his chest.

Oland died of natural causes in February 1957. He was seventy-one.

Michael Betts, whose story to police as a five-year-old led to Oland's arrest and trial, died of cancer at age twenty-six in 1919.

Antonio "Andy" Miller lies in an unmarked grave in Muncie's Beech Grove Cemetery. Surviving records don't indicate exactly where he was laid to rest. His slaying was never solved.

The Hoosier Thunderbolt and the Muncie Freak

One was baseball's first great fastball pitcher, a man whose mound skills changed the national pastime forever and earned him a place in its Hall of Fame. The other was a self-proclaimed freak, boasting of his ability to cheat death despite routinely having spikes driven into his skull, being buried underground in quasi-coffins for stretches of several days and consuming poison and live snakes.

Both spent some turbulent periods of their lives—in part due to marital misadventures—in Muncie.

Amos Rusie, the "Hoosier Thunderbolt," was a star pitcher for the New York Giants in the 1890s, at one point winning at least thirty-two games in four consecutive seasons.

His speed and occasional lack of control were apparently key components in a decision to increase the distance from the pitcher's mound to home plate—from fifty feet to the still standard sixty feet, six inches—in 1893.

One of Rusie's pitching contemporaries, the far better remembered Cy Young, always ranked the Hoosier among the greatest hurlers he ever saw.

When a Reading, Pennsylvania reporter praised Young's fastball in 1909, the pitcher responded, "I guess you never saw Amos Rusie. My fastball looks like a slow freight trying to keep up with the Pennsylvania Limited compared to Rusie's."

The Mooresville native's pitching exploits aside, Rusie's career with the Giants was also marked by conflicts with team management and disputes over his pay, setting the stage for salary holdouts that, at times combined with arm woes, saw him skip entire seasons.

Those missed seasons were likely fine with the pitching ace's wife, the former Susie May Sloan of Muncie.

The couple was married in Delaware County in 1890, after Rusie's first season with the Giants, and apparently frequently spent the off-seasons with her relatives in Muncie.

In December 1896, the *Wilmington (NC) Morning Star* reported that Rusie was staying at the home of his in-laws in Muncie, enjoying hunting in the area, when he signed a $4,000 contract to pitch for the Giants in 1897 after sitting out the previous season.

As the nineteenth century wound to a close, both Rusie's career—he would again sit out both the 1899 and 1900 seasons—and his marriage were in turmoil.

After a baseball career that would earn him a place in the Hall of Fame, star pitcher Amos Rusie saved his troubled marriage by moving to Muncie. *Courtesy of the Library of Congress.*

Rusie was apparently planning to pitch for the Giants in 1900, but that March, his wife—who didn't like the temptations his celebrity status in New York City created for her husband—left him, returning to Muncie to stay with relatives, Mr. and Mrs. Bert Cupp.

Her husband followed her west but apparently remained in Indianapolis. The pitcher's sudden departure from New York made headlines there.

On April 18, the Cupps confirmed that Mrs. Rusie intended to file for divorce in Marion County, charging her husband with cruel and inhumane treatment.

At a May 4 hearing in Indianapolis, Susie May Rusie was granted her divorce—"under sensational circumstances," the *Pittsburgh Post* reported—and was awarded the couple's furniture and a $1,000 alimony payment.

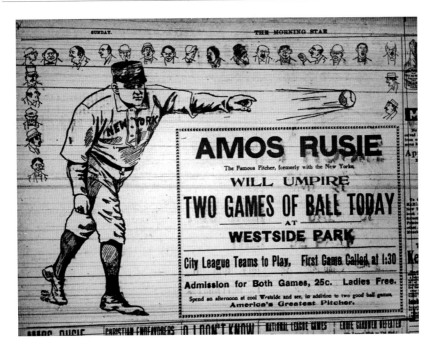

Soon after Rusie relocated to Muncie for good, local officials persuaded him to umpire a pair of city-league games at Westside Park. *Courtesy of the* Muncie Morning Star.

Amos Rusie came into the courtroom, intoxicated and armed with a revolver, and was ordered to leave after he "leaned over the back of his wife's chair and attempted to begin a conversation with her."

"Mrs. Rusie jumped from her chair in terror and ran directly to the judge, saying Amos had threatened to kill her," the *Chicago Inter Ocean* reported.

Upon her return to Muncie that night, Mrs. Rusie asked city police for special protection, saying she believed "her husband followed her to Muncie and will try to kill her," the *Brooklyn Daily Eagle* told its readers.

The divorce didn't stick.

On July 31, Rusie picked up Susie May at her relatives' home in Muncie, and the couple drove to Grant County, where they were remarried.

News accounts indicated the pitcher had agreed to his wife's demand that he "abandon the diamond."

The reconciled couple would settle into a home in the city's south-side Congerville neighborhood.

A few weeks later, Amos was back on the diamond, however—the diamond at Muncie's Westside Park, where newspaper ads announced he would "umpire two games of ball" featuring city-league teams.

For twenty-five cents, fans could watch both games and see "America's greatest pitcher."

Soon, rumors of a Rusie pitching comeback—albeit closer to home than New York City—began to surface.

Rusie's brother-in-law, John Smith, told the *Muncie Morning Star* in September 1900 that the pitcher intended to play for the Cincinnati Reds in 1901 and also would be opening a tavern in Muncie.

The tavern never materialized, but that December, the Giants did send Rusie to the Reds in a trade for a then-unknown young hurler named Christy Mathewson.

It would prove to be one of the worst trades, from Cincinnati's perspective, in baseball history.

Mathewson over the next sixteen seasons won 373 games for the Giants, leading them to five National League pennants.

Rusie pitched all of three games for the Reds before returning to Muncie, expressing unhappiness with the amount of time he was given to work his arm back into shape.

While there would continue to be reports of a planned comeback, Amos Rusie's major-league pitching career was over. He was thirty years old.

For the next several years, sports columnists would travel to Muncie to provide their readers with updates on what the game's once most-revered pitcher was up to, at times in a mocking manner.

"Upon first blush, the story of the fall of the mightiest baseball pitcher the world ever knew—Amos Rusie—from his $4,000-a-year position to that of a day laborer, digging ditches for a Muncie, Ind., waterworks company, seems to be the acme of pathetic in the world of athletics," the *Louisville Courier-Journal* reported in December 1901.

The story noted, though, that Rusie and his wife were far happier with a more sedate lifestyle.

"I'm leading a good, clean, honest life, and I am the last to need any pity," Rusie said.

Mrs. Rusie said her husband's time in New York had provided "the most unhappy hours of my life."

Also that month, the *Boston Post* reported Rusie was earning about twenty cents per hour as a trench digger in Muncie.

"Yet the passing of the famous twirler has been gradual," it added. "His friends foresaw the trench digger in the pitcher years ago.

"Whisky did it."

The most bizarre post-baseball Rusie story was published in the *Indianapolis Star* in June 1906. It reported that the former ballplayer lived with his family at a campsite along the Wabash River near Vincennes and was now a "full-fledged mussel shell digger."

Rusie would later deny the widespread shell-digging claims.

In 1910, the *Eau Claire (WI) Leader* reported Rusie was "a hardworking lumberman in Muncie, Ind., and not a pearl diver at $1.50 a day, as has been reported many times."

About that time, the Rusies and their daughter left Muncie for Seattle, Washington, where Amos found work in a shipyard.

In 1921, there was an unlikely return to the New York Giants. This time, Rusie hired on as superintendent of the Polo Grounds, a job he held for eight years.

He and Susie May then returned to Seattle, this time for good. They died there, eight weeks apart, in 1942.

Except for that brief, highly publicized divorce in 1900, they had been married for fifty-two years.

More than three decades after his death, in 1977, Rusie was finally elected to the National Baseball Hall of Fame by its veterans' committee. He was

Death-defying performer Harry Beno, for a time known as "the Muncie freak," was a featured attraction at fairs and carnivals around the turn of the century. *Courtesy of the Library of Congress.*

represented at the induction ceremony by his nephew and namesake John Amos Rusie, a former Miami County sheriff.

Not named posthumously to a Hall of Fame—although perhaps he should have been—was Harry Beno, for a time known as "the Muncie freak."

Beno, who claimed to be the son of an English mother and Egyptian father, was frequently in the headlines around the turn of the century—both in east-central Indiana and throughout the Midwest—due to his various stunts.

They included being buried alive for up to twelve days, allowing people to drive "a shoemaker's awl [into] the top of his skull a half-inch deep" and consuming poison and live reptiles.

"Beno is a freak," physician J.F. Binnie—who removed a steel nail that had become lodged in the entertainer's skull in March 1900—told the *Kansas City Star*. "Either he is a man with nerve to suffer pain without flinching or else his nervous system is so blunted as to be devoid of sensation."

The physician reported finding "half a score of punctures in Beno's skull, made by nails which he had driven in while giving exhibitions."

The *Oamaru Mail*, a newspaper in New Zealand, said Beno had "discovered his remarkable gift" several years earlier while in Richmond, Indiana, when he "ate by mistake a piece of bread which had been thoroughly saturated with strychnine for the purpose of poisoning rats."

For a time, he traveled with side shows as "the poison king…swallowing doses of the most deadly poisons." He would later develop other death-defying stunts.

On July 5, 1898, Beno was "dug up" after being buried in a coffin-like box for eight days, without food and water, "in the center of the arena at the Maple Grove garden," the *Muncie Morning News* reported.

The newspaper said Beno appeared to emerge from a trance soon after being brought above ground and then ate a cracker.

The "freak of nature" apparently won $100 in a wager with another newspaper, which had suggested his stunt would prove bogus.

While underground, Beno had spoken to curious Muncie citizens "through the tube that furnishes fresh air to him," the *News* reported.

Some of those conversations were apparently with Muncie resident Grace Waymer.

Upon his return from the grave, Beno proposed marriage, and Waymer accepted. The couple wed that week, county marriage records confirm.

But within a month, the marriage was on the rocks, news accounts suggest.

On August 17, the *Hagerstown Exponent* said Mrs. Beno had "abandoned her freakish husband and returned home" to Muncie.

"Miss Waymer fell in love with the man, and after he was buried she visited his grave regularly, bringing fresh flowers," the story said. "They have since traveled together."

The *Exponent* detailed two reasons for the newlyweds' marital woes: Grace had determined Beno seemed very focused on drawing publicity and attention. "Another discovery the woman made was that Beno has a disposition to sleep all the time [and] consequently is poor company."

Beno sightings continued in the Midwest for a few years. There were also occasionally bogus accounts of his death.

In December 1899, he was reported to have died in Union Point, Georgia, by the *Daily Review* of Decatur, Illinois, which fondly recalled Beno being buried alive during that city's most recent "corn carnival."

That article said Grace Waymer Beno, apparently still married to the entertainer, was en route from Muncie to Georgia.

"Our carnival freak to be buried for good," the headline read. "His wife was a Muncie girl who loved him."

Subsequent articles, however, reflect that report of Beno's death was premature.

In August 1902, he arrived in Joplin, Missouri, "with a nail protruding from the top of his head" and "asked to be shown to a machine shop instead of the hospital," the *Topeka (KS) Daily Capital* reported.

That article said he was "known the world over as 'The Doctor's Puzzle.'"

The previous May, he had been run out of Topeka after being charged with vagrancy. About a week earlier, he had been buried for seventy-two hours near an intersection there.

The Beno saga ended sadly in November 1903, when he was reported to have died after lingering for three months in a Kansas City hospital. This time, the reports of his passing appear to have been true.

"Man with sponge head passes away," a headline in the *Marion (OH) Star* read.

According to the *St. Paul (MN) Globe*, "Beno the Wonder" has been paralyzed since he struck an awl with too much force at a performance in southern Missouri, piercing his brain.

"Nearly his whole life had been spent in the show business and he had traveled with many of the large circuses," that report said.

A eulogy in the *Minneapolis Journal* would pay tribute to the former Muncie resident's "glorious life work." "Many a man has said that if he could see Beno puncture his head with an awl he would not take a ticket to a public hanging," the writer concluded. "Surely a life like this has not been lived in vain."

A Police Commissioner
Goes Up the River

As a police commissioner for Mayor Rollin Bunch, Xene Young Smith helped oversee law enforcement in Muncie from 1914 to 1919.

During those years, Bunch and Smith—both local physicians—found themselves the frequent targets of investigations by local grand juries and federal authorities.

The allegations usually centered on claims of corruption, including the pursuit of "protection money" from what one news account called "gamblers, resort keepers and 'blind tiger' operators in Muncie."

In 1919, Bunch's second term as mayor came to an abrupt end when a federal jury found him guilty of mail fraud.

Bunch, a Democrat, maintained that his support for labor unions had resulted in a well-known group of local industrialists using their connections to engineer his downfall. He was sentenced to two years in federal prison but served only a few months before being pardoned by President Woodrow Wilson.

No one knew it at the time, but "Doc" Bunch's colleague Xene Smith was also destined for prison—in a case that involved far more serious allegations than any ever lodged against the former mayor.

On the early morning of Friday, June 10, 1921, a buggy occupied by two local Romanian immigrants, cousins Costan "Gus" and Gabriel Voida, was traveling on the Macedonia Pike southeast of Muncie when it was approached at a dark intersection by what police at first referred to as a gang of "highwaymen."

Muncie mayor Rollin Bunch, who appointed fellow physician Xene Smith as police commissioner, served a brief federal prison term for a corruption-related conviction. *Courtesy of Ball State University archives.*

The Voidas would tell police they ignored a demand to stop their buggy and then became the targets of a flurry of gunshots as they raced away.

One .25-caliber bullet tore through the rear of the buggy and struck Gus Voida in his back, piercing his stomach and intestines.

Gabriel Voida dropped off his badly wounded cousin at Home Hospital on Muncie's south side, where he underwent surgery to remove the bullet.

Newspaper accounts indicate that police investigating the shooting at first focused on Muncie's "Little Romania colony" on the city's southeast side, then made up of about fifty immigrants.

A police "cleanup" of the area resulted in raids at a Perry Township farmhouse the Voidas had apparently visited on the night of the shooting and an East Tenth Street house where officers confiscated several gallons of liquor and a barrel of "mash."

Prohibition had gone into effect eighteen months earlier, in January 1920, and two members of the "colony"—one of them Gabriel Voida—were sentenced that week to 120 days at the State Farm for liquor law violations.

Gus Voida lingered in Home Hospital until Wednesday, June 15, when he died of peritonitis. The thirty-one-year-old victim would be buried in his adopted hometown's Beech Grove Cemetery.

Before he died, however, Voida was able to give police clues about the events that led to the attempted robbery and his shooting.

He was also able to identify a photograph of a man he met with several hours before the attack who had asked to buy thirty gallons of bootleg whiskey, the product of "a still in which Voida had an interest," the *Indianapolis News* reported.

The photograph was of Xene Smith, physician and former city police commissioner.

"That's the man!" the shooting victim told detectives. "Can you get him?"

Smith had moved to Indianapolis since his service as a police commissioner ended but still spent much of his time in Muncie, keeping an apartment in the 500 block of South Walnut Street.

Police that week arrested Smith, Muncie horse trainer Ross Keith and James Mabrey, described as a "police character," in the robbery conspiracy that led to Voida's death.

Muncie Doctor Pleads Guilty to Manslaughter

Dr. Xene Y. Smith.

Winchester, Ind., Nov. 9.—Dr. Xene Y. Smith, of Muncie, who pleaded guilty today in the Randolph County Circuit Court to a charge of manslaughter in connection with the murder of Gus Voida, will probably be taken to the Indiana state prison on Monday.

Physician Xene Smith, an ex–Muncie police commissioner, was convicted of manslaughter in a robbery plot that led to a local man's murder. *Courtesy of the* Muncie Star.

On June 23, a grand jury indicted the men on first-degree murder charges. A fourth co-defendant, Carl "Tommy" Teague, a "lightweight pugilist of Muncie," was charged with conspiracy to commit robbery.

Because of pre-trial publicity, a Delaware County judge agreed to transfer the cases to surrounding counties in east-central Indiana.

Smith, then forty-four, was scheduled to be the first to stand trial that November in Randolph Circuit Court. However, those proceedings came to an abrupt end when the physician struck a deal with prosecutors, pleading guilty to manslaughter in exchange for the dismissal of the murder charge.

Smith—sentenced to two to twenty-one years in the state prison—acknowledged that the fatal shooting took place during an "attempt to steal illicit whisky from two Romanians," the *Logansport Morning News* reported.

In testimony at his sentencing hearing, Smith implicated his three co-defendants and a fifth alleged conspirator, twenty-four-year-old Glen "Big Foot" Zoll.

Later that month, all five men charged in the scheme would testify as Keith stood trial on murder and robbery counts in Madison County.

The testimony about the night of the shooting was inconsistent, to say the least:

* Smith—returned from the state prison in Michigan City to testify—told the Madison County jury it was Keith who had fired a .25-caliber handgun "point-blank" into the buggy that night. The physician also maintained that the Voidas had opened fire with their own guns after the conspirators tried to stop their buggy.

"I did not know anyone had been hurt until I read of Voida's death in the newspapers," Smith said. "It was too dark to see anything that occurred."

* Mabrey, however, insisted the Voidas had fired no gunshots. He and Keith both testified that they were unarmed that night and were unaware of the plan to rob the cousins of their whiskey.

Mabrey also said Smith had told him, "The damned Hunkies [an ethnic slur of the time referring to Eastern Europeans] didn't stop and I gave them a good scare."

* Keith told the jurors deciding his fate that he had been paid twenty-five dollars to accompany Smith and the others to a rural address to pick up whiskey, not to commit a robbery. He also said the day after he, Mabrey and Smith were arrested, the physician told them, "Boys, I did it. I am in for it."

* The twenty-four-year-old Zoll—at the time awaiting trial on a robbery charge stemming from an earlier holdup at a Union City gambling house—maintained he had fired no shots.

* Teague, meanwhile, gave an entirely different account of the events. He said Smith, in a meeting of conspirators at Liberty Street and the Big Four railroad crossings, had told him of the plan to rob the Voidas "of white mule whiskey and make some money."

The twenty-one-year-old boxer said Smith and Mabrey had met earlier that day with Gus Voida in a South Walnut Street restaurant and made a deal to buy thirty gallons of whiskey in jugs supplied by the conspirators. They anticipated finding that whiskey, and taking it without paying the suppliers, after intercepting the Voidas on Macedonia Pike that night.

* Gabriel Voida took the witness stand and denied that he and his cousin were armed that night. He said while dying in the hospital, Gus told him he believed Smith had shot him.

The Madison Circuit Court jury deliberated for four hours before finding Keith not guilty of murder and conspiracy to commit robbery.

Several in the courtroom gallery, reportedly Muncie associates of Keith, cheered and applauded when Judge William A. Kittinger read the verdicts.

The judge was livid and hinted that jury tampering had taken place.

"Such a verdict places a premium on crime, and it would be poetic justice if every member of this jury were held up on the way home and shot at by the same kind of fellows who were mixed up in the Muncie murder," he said.

A few minutes later, a sheriff's deputy asked Judge Kittinger what should be done with Keith, who was shaking hands with members of the jury, the *Greenfield Daily Reporter* said.

"Turn him loose and let him go back to Muncie," the judge snapped. "I don't care what you do with him."

Kittinger later called the verdicts "a disgrace to the good citizenship of Madison County" and said members of the jury would never serve that role in his court again.

Delaware County prosecutor Clarence Bendaum called the outcome of the Keith trial "the biggest farce I have encountered during my experience as an attorney."

In January, the *Indianapolis Star* reported that a Delaware County grand jury might conduct further investigation of the Voida killing.

A few days earlier, a Henry County judge had agreed to throw the indictments against Mabrey out of court.

(Soon after Keith's acquittal, Mabrey testified in Indianapolis at yet another federal trial stemming from allegations of corruption in Muncie. Mabrey told that jury he had earlier operated a "liquor establishment" in Muncie and paid city officials ten dollars a week for "protection." He said he also collected such payments from other businessmen and turned the cash over to then–police commissioner Smith, who assured him the money went to "higher ups.")

Teague and Zoll would also never stand trial on the conspiracy to commit robbery charges.

(Teague, at one point rumored to be in line for a bout against lightweight champion Benny Leonard, would die of a respiratory illness in December 1923. Zoll—who would have other scrapes with the law—was seventy-four when he died in Muncie in 1973.)

In March 1923, Gus Voida's widow, Florence, filed a lawsuit demanding $10,000 from the five men who had been charged in her husband's death.

Also that year, physician Smith was released after serving a minimum two-year sentence for his role in the killing. He apparently at that point retired from the medical profession and moved to a Randolph County farm just north of Union City.

Xene Smith was sixty-five when he died of a sudden heart attack while dressing a chicken in his yard on March 21, 1942. His body was returned to Muncie—where his old friend "Doc" Bunch, a few weeks later, would win the Democratic nomination in yet another campaign for mayor—for burial in Elm Ridge Cemetery.

Smith's obituary noted his past public service as a Muncie police commissioner but made no reference to the unpleasant events of 1921.

6

THE SAD SAGA OF
MUNCIE'S HOLLAND TRIPLETS

They were almost certainly Muncie's most famous triplets. Their birth and childhoods were marked by fame on a national level.

But more than four decades later, one of the Holland triplets was involved in a headline-making scandal that brought her a new and unwanted amount of notoriety.

In May 1935, Mrs. William Holland of Muncie gave birth to triplets. The girls, all born within an hour, were delivered at the family's home in the 1100 block of East Jackson Street.

The birth of triplets was not common in Muncie; African American triplets like the Hollands were even rarer, and by some accounts, the Holland girls were Muncie's first.

Triplets of any race were big enough news in Muncie that newspapers did stories about their births. When the Erbaugh triplets were born in September 1956, an article noted they were the first since 1951.

A 1954 article noted the birthday of the two surviving members of the Thompsons, believed to be Muncie's first set of triplets. They were born in July 1904, although the article noted that the third was stillborn.

A *Muncie Evening Press* article from 1972 noted that fourteen sets of triplets had been born in Muncie up until that time.

"The oldest triplets still living in Muncie are June, Joan and Jean, three of the eight children of William Holland," the article noted.

The Holland triplets. *Courtesy of Ball State University archives.*

Born May 10, 1935, they were unusually close to each other. Joan looked like her mother and the other two, who were identical, like their father. Seldom separated until they were 19, they often sang in churches and elsewhere.

Central High School graduates, they traveled a lot later, to Hawaii, to Germany, etc., where servicemen husbands of the girls were stationed. "America's a beautiful country," says Joan. "Nobody owes you a thing. God helps you if you help yourself, and we've worked hard."

When the Holland triplets were born in 1935, the world was fascinated by multiple births. In May 1934, the Dionne quintuplets were born in Canada.

The Dionne name was even cited in newspapers at the time of the Holland triplets' birth, as William Holland took an unusual step toward fame for his offspring.

"Mrs. Dionne's Rival May Ask First Lady to Name Triplets," read the headline in the *Pittsburgh (PA) Courier.*

"Mrs. Roosevelt asked to name triplet girls," was the headline in the *Edinburg (IN) Daily Courier.*

Indeed, William Holland had asked Muncie mayor Rollin Bunch—"who has taken an interest in the babies"—to "request Mrs. Roosevelt to suggest names for them."

There's nothing to indicate that Eleanor Roosevelt actually suggested the names June, Joan and Jean.

In a 1994 article in the *Muncie Star*, a columnist asked readers if they had any idea what had happened to the Holland triplets.

Strangely enough, a check of the newspaper's own archive would have revealed what happened to June Holland, at least. It's possible, however, that the outcome of her story was so improbable as to seem unbelievable.

In 1981, June Holland was charged with killing her neighbor.

On March 1 of that year, Holland was arrested after the death of her neighbor, seventy-eight-year-old Hilda Niedenthal.

Holland—who, police said at the time of her arrest, had spent time in a mental institution in the past—went to her neighbor to ask if she could buy her home. Holland left when she was told the house was not for sale but returned with a board and struck the elderly woman.

Delaware Superior Court judge Robert Barnet Jr. *Courtesy of Muncie Newspapers Inc.*

Delaware County coroner Larry Cole said Niedenthal suffered a skull fracture and died from a blood clot that formed when her head struck concrete pavement after the fall from the blow.

A formal charge of murder was filed, and Holland was held in the Delaware County jail.

Delaware Superior Court judge Robert Barnet Jr. appointed two psychiatrists to examine Holland.

In May 1981, Barnet ruled that Holland was not competent to stand trial. The judge said Holland was not able to understand the charges against her or aid in her own defense.

"Miss Holland shouted obscenities at her attorney and the judge during a brief court appearance," the *Muncie Star* reported.

Holland was sent to the Richmond State Hospital for evaluation, however, and another twist in her case followed.

In an August 1981 hearing, Barnet judged Holland competent to stand trial. She had, since the May court hearing, been examined by two more court-appointed psychiatrists and judged fit for trial.

At stake was her future and her freedom. If convicted of murder, Holland would face twenty years in prison.

Holland was put on trial in November 1981. During that trial, the daughter of the woman killed earlier that year testified that Holland, after being refused the opportunity to purchase her neighbor's house, stood in the backyard, screaming profanities.

Niedenthal and her daughter were leaving the house to get in a car when Holland hit her elderly neighbor in the head with a board or club.

"I couldn't believe this was happening," the victim's daughter told a jury of seven men and five women.

Adding to the tragic circumstances: the woman said her father had died from a head injury from a fall in the same spot two years earlier.

Holland's circumstances leading up to the trial were also tragic. One of her fellow triplets had died a few years before Holland's trial, and the other died during the criminal proceedings. The girls' mother had died when they were ten years old, and their father died three years before June Holland was charged with murder.

June's life, authorities said, was marked by upset and turmoil. The girls were pulled out of school in the eleventh grade. June said she considered herself a loner with only one close friend.

She married at age twenty-one, she said, only to find out that the man she married already had a wife. Several marriages followed, and so did hospitalizations for mental illness. During preparation for her trial, she said one husband drove her insane.

Police said they quickly came to believe that Holland was not in her right mind. Besides her confusion, she seemed unable to grasp the seriousness of her situation, instead commenting on how beautiful the room at police headquarters was during her questioning.

Holland's brother told police that his sister had "mental problems" throughout her life and that she kept seventeen cats and "seven or eight" dogs in her home.

Psychiatrists hired by defense attorney Jack Quirk testified that Holland suffered from chronic mental illness, including schizophrenia.

Holland did not testify and sat motionless throughout her trial.

"It comes down to whether you believe people like June Holland should be put in a penal institution—a prison—or a mental institution," Quirk said.

After deliberating for less than an hour, a jury found June Holland not guilty by reason of insanity in the killing of her neighbor.

Defense attorney Quirk had argued that while his client was insane, it would be "a mistake" to free her, adding that she "needs treatment from somebody that knows what they're doing."

But a prison sentence meant that she would be "the butt of everyone's jokes." A few days after her trial ended, Barnet committed Holland to the Richmond State Hospital. She would stay there until he decided otherwise.

Although the murder case against Holland was covered extensively by local newspapers, the columnist who wrote about triplets, and specifically the Hollands, in 1994 didn't make the connection.

"There is no listing for any of the triplets in the 1994 Muncie telephone book," the newspaper reported and urged anyone with information about the Holland girls to contact a local historian.

Court records indicate Holland was released from the hospital a decade after her crime and lived in transitional housing for the mentally ill. She died in 2003 at age sixty-seven.

Unlike her birth, her death did not make headlines.

7

The Death of a Chicken Thief

It wasn't the first time lawmen had an encounter with Jess O'Geese. But on this morning in May 1954, it would be the last. And it was a decidedly one-sided meeting, as O'Geese lay dead on the ground outside a farmer's chicken coop while officers stood over his body.

O'Geese had lived in Muncie for more than thirty years, making headlines as early as 1923 on a decidedly happier occasion. But this time, O'Geese's police mug shot, leftover from a previous arrest, appeared alongside the story of his sudden and violent death—a story that had a final twist.

O'Geese was born about 1881 and was a paperhanger by trade, putting up wallpaper in homes and businesses. Newspaper accounts at the time of his death at age seventy-three don't say where he was from but note that he was arrested for larceny in Columbus, Ohio, in 1914. Since that time, he had made his way around Indiana, with arrests in Greencastle, Madison, Seymour and Pendleton.

On November 9, 1923, O'Geese made headlines on page two of the *Muncie Post-Democrat*. Newspaper publisher George Dale's muckraking broadsheet took on the powerful and moneyed interests that ran Muncie for much of the first part of the twentieth century: the Ku Klux Klan and corrupt politicians.

The headline that day in 1923 proclaimed, "Jess O'Geese Wins Price of Fine Shooting African Golluf at Bob Graves Protected Haven."

Dale's headline is a bit of a puzzler now, but at the time, in-the-know Muncie residents quickly understood that a black man had won a lot of money on a dice game in a local gambling house.

The *Post-Democrat* was known for reflecting the views of its publisher. The stories on page one of this November day's edition called the local Democratic Party chairman a "klucker" and warned that local KKK members sought the removal of a Catholic teacher from Muncie schools. The teacher was considered "fair game for the cowards who disport themselves in cornfields at night, clad in nightgowns with pillow cases over their heads," the newspaper article noted.

So publisher Dale—who would be elected to the Muncie mayor's office in 1929—no doubt took some delight in reporting that O'Geese, a black man, had won big in gambling the night before.

The newspaper recounted how O'Geese came to a "protected gambling house and blind pig" on South Walnut Street. Prohibition—the national ban on alcoholic beverages that lasted from 1920 to 1933—was in full swing in 1923, and speakeasies (also known as blind pigs) were "underground" bars where the public could drink.

Exonerate Randolph Farmer in Shooting

Jess O'Geese, 73, of 717 S. Pershing Dr., was shot and fatally injured by Leonard Slusher, a Randolph County farmer who lives near Stoney Creek, early Thursday when Slusher apprehended the Muncie man near his chicken house.

According to Sheriff Cliff Hines, O'Geese was killed instantly during a scuffle with the farmer who lives six miles southwest of Farmland. The shooting took place about 2 a.m.

Sheriff Hines and Dr. Harvey White of Farmland, county coroner, said no charges would be filed against Slusher and that no grand jury action would be taken.

O'Geese, who had been questioned previously about stealing chickens in Randolph County, and who also had been arrested in Muncie, Greencastle, Madison, Seymour and Pendleton, was said by local police to have supplied hens to so-called "chicken shacks" in Muncie for a number of years.

His police record dates back to Oct. 20, 1914, when he was arrested at Columbus, O., for larceny. He last was arrested in Muncie Nov. 15, 1953 for driving while under the influence of intoxicants. He was acquitted of the charge last Feb. 25.

Had Sack Full of Chickens

Sheriff Hines and Deputy Leo Hubbard, who investigated the shooting, said O'Geese was carrying a burlap sack full of chickens when Slusher rounded the brooder house and accosted him. Hubbard said there was an exchange of words, and then O'Geese attempted to distract Slusher's attention.

"I guess you got me," O'Geese said, according to the farmer. Then he pointed beyond Slusher and said, "My buddy's right down there."

When Slusher half turned to look, O'Geese made a grab for the gun, according to the story told the sheriff's officers, and the two wrestled briefly for the weapon. Then Slusher yanked it around

Muncie Police Photo

JESS O'GEESE

widow, Hazel; three stepdaughters, Henrietta and Nellie Warner, and Stella Mae Speaks, and two nieces, Lena and Thelma Jones of Cincinnati.

Jess O'Geese in an undated police mug shot. *Courtesy of Muncie Newspapers Inc.*

O'Geese, whom the newspaper reported was out on bond pending a liquor-related charge, "pulled off some real comedy."

"Jess walked into the gambling house and laid one hundred thirty dollars on the crap table," the *Post-Democrat* reported. He massaged the "bones" (the dice) between his hands.

(O'Geese was playing dice, although the headline reference to "African Golluf" was apparently a joke; golluf was a parlor game, similar to table tennis, popular in the early 1900s.)

The newspaper reported that O'Geese rolled the dice and came up with eleven, winning a pot of $800.

Although publisher Dale plainly disagreed, the article noted that a special judge had given the gambling house and speakeasy "a clean bill of health" not many days before.

That meant, the *Post-Democrat* noted, that O'Geese could use his gambling windfall to settle his legal troubles.

"Jess's fine is paid and he got it lawfully, for the judge held that Bob isn't running a gambling house," the article noted.

O'Geese would continue, over the next few decades, to be well known to local police and newspaper readers.

The 1954 article reporting his violent death noted that he was facing a Muncie City Court charge of driving while intoxicated. He had been acquitted of a similar charge in early 1953.

There was no hope of acquittal for O'Geese in May 1954, however, and justice—at least as far as police saw it—came quickly.

In the twenty-first century, the African American population of Randolph County—one county to the east of Muncie and Delaware County—is less than 1 percent of the population as a whole. Although history tells us there were black settlements in Randolph County in the mid-1800s, it's safe to say that residents of the rural county were wary of black men on their property in the spring of 1954.

Just before 2:00 a.m. on Thursday, May 27, Randolph County farmer Leonard Slusher and his wife were awakened by their granddaughter, who was staying with them, asking for a glass of water.

When she went to get the water, Mrs. Slusher looked out a window and saw car headlights blink off on the road near their house, six miles south of the town of Farmland. She told her husband.

"Slusher had been having trouble with chicken thieves recently and had made a practice of leaving a light on in his hen house," the *Muncie Evening Press* reported in its afternoon edition, coming out about twelve hours after the incident.

Farmer Slusher grabbed his twelve-gauge shotgun and went out into the barn lot.

As Slusher approached the chicken house, the light went out. The farmer shone his own light into the house and saw O'Geese with a sack in his hands.

"I guess you got me," O'Geese said, according to Slusher's account. "My buddy's right down there."

As the farmer turned to look, he told police, O'Geese tried to grab his gun. Slusher recovered, aimed the shotgun at O'Geese and pulled the trigger.

An Indiana chicken coop. *Courtesy of the Library of Congress.*

The blast not only severed O'Geese's right thumb but also hit O'Geese's right thigh, causing major blood loss.

Randolph County sheriff Cliff Hines was called, as were Muncie police, who quickly accepted the farmer's account and believed the dead man's guilt. As reported in the *Muncie Evening Press* the same day as the shooting:

O'Geese had supplied hens for so-called "chicken shacks" [in Muncie] for a number of years.

O'Geese had been arrested before in Randolph County [and] he had also been questioned at Richmond and at Anderson regarding chicken thefts.

Sheriff Hines said O'Geese was carrying a burlap sack of chickens when the farmer confronted him and that two more burlap sacks were found near the car.

"The man had white shoe strings in his pockets, which he apparently used to tie the sacks," Randolph County coroner Harvey White said. Feathers were found in O'Geese's car trunk.

"Apparently he had made forages before," White said.

The burlap sacks, chickens and feathers were sufficient to convince authorities of O'Geese's intent.

But what of Farmer Slusher, who shot O'Geese to death? Authorities very quickly determined that the farmer was justified in using deadly force to protect his chickens.

In the *Muncie Star*'s story on the incident, published just twenty-four hours later, the decision was already made. Although it was standard practice in Indiana in the 1950s to take homicides to legally empaneled grand juries to determine if a charge of murder would be filed, authorities said they didn't believe it was necessary in this case.

"Exonerate Randolph Farmer in Shooting," the headline read.

"Sheriff Hines and Dr. Harvey Wright of Farmland, county coroner, said no charges would be filed against Slusher and that no grand jury action would be taken," the article noted.

A total of two articles, one in each of Muncie's newspapers, were written about the incident.

The next day's papers had one-paragraph obituaries for O'Geese, "who was shot and fatally wounded early Thursday by a Randolph County farmer." Funeral services were held a few days later.

Jess O'Geese, who had made headlines for his good fortune in a dice game three decades before, made headlines again for his ill fortune in a rural county where chicken thieves received harsh treatment and where other potential victims no doubt felt encouraged and emboldened to defend themselves and their feathery flocks.

8

Farmer in the Well and the Dance of Death

A *Muncie Evening Press* headline proclaimed it an "unnatural crime with few parallels in criminal history." Whether or not it met that standard, twenty-two-year-old Benjamin Harrison Smith's killing of his father, Charles, was decidedly unpleasant.

On the night of November 17, 1910, the younger Smith, who lived with his family along the Bethel Pike about four miles northwest of Muncie, went to a neighbor's home to report he had just been assaulted by two masked "highwaymen."

He also said the bandits had apparently commandeered his father's horse and buggy and had perhaps done him in as well.

Muncie police and Delaware County sheriff's deputies searched the area for Charles V. Smith, who would have celebrated his sixty-ninth birthday later that week.

He was nowhere to be found. Noting some inconsistencies in young Ben's story, investigators "sweated" him, news accounts said, and he eventually told them what had really unfolded.

Charles Smith had informed his son—later described by the *Evening Press* as a "shiftless and worthless fellow"—that he needed to find work and begin paying two dollars a week for his room and board.

Angry words were exchanged, Ben Smith said, and his father tossed a brick that struck the son in the shoulder.

The younger Smith picked up the brick and repeatedly struck his father in the head with it, inflicting injuries that he at first believed to be fatal.

This *Muncie Morning Star* illustration shows killer Benjamin Harrison Smith; his father and victim, Charles; and key locations in the events leading up to the brutal slaying. *Courtesy of the* Muncie Morning Star.

The son pulled his victim into the buggy and set off for a nearby farm owned by the Petty family. Its farmhouse was unoccupied. It also had a well.

Unfortunately for Charles Smith, he had survived his son's initial attack. He began to regain consciousness on the buggy ride down Bethel Pike. This time, his son was armed with a monkey wrench, and he beat his groaning father in the head, again and again.

Once at the Petty farm, Ben dragged his mortally injured victim out of the buggy and threw him, head first, down the well.

Searchers who later recovered the body said the well was only about fifteen feet deep, and the water was so shallow that the victim's feet were not submerged.

Charles Smith—who had moved with his family from Kentucky to Delaware County about fifteen years earlier—wore "long whiskers," authorities said, and his beard had been stained red by the bloody well water.

An autopsy would confirm he suffered at least a dozen skull fractures, and authorities could not rule out that he had died as a result of drowning in the well.

Nine days after the slaying, a Delaware County grand jury indicted Benjamin Harrison Smith on a charge of first-degree murder. There was speculation that he might receive the first death sentence in county history.

At an initial hearing on November 30, however, he entered a guilty plea. The next day, Judge Frank Ellis, a former Muncie mayor, sentenced Smith to life in prison.

His stay in prison would be a short one. On February 16, 1911, seventy-five days after he was delivered to the state prison in Michigan City, Ben Smith used a pair of suspenders to hang himself from an overhead pipe in his cell.

A dozen weeks earlier, Charles Smith—the father of fourteen children, including his killer—had been laid to rest in Beech Grove Cemetery.

Ben would not join him there. His remains were interred at the cemetery at the state prison.

The defendant in another high-profile murder case of that era, if nothing else, enjoyed a much better relationship with his father.

Charles V. McGalliard Jr., twenty-six, was reportedly intoxicated, deranged or both when he fatally shot his girlfriend, Alta Hayworth, during a masked ball on Halloween 1911. As many as two hundred revelers witnessed the slaying.

The murder—which attracted statewide headlines and became known as the "Dance of Death" killing—took place at Franklin Hall, at Mulberry and Washington Streets.

The twenty-one-year-old victim was shot in the lungs and heart as she waltzed—and apparently argued—with McGalliard. Hayworth staggered a short distance, cried, "Oh, I'm shot!" and collapsed.

In the wake of her death, the Muncie Police Board prohibited public dances. (A witness to the shooting had died of a heart attack later that night, and news coverage that revealed her husband was at the dance without her prompted a Muncie woman to file for divorce.)

Murderer in "the Dance of Death" and His Victim

CHARLES M'GALLIARD, JR.   MISS ALTA HAYWORTH

DEATH DANCE   **SEQUESTERED TAXES FOUND**

Charles McGalliard Jr. fatally shot his dancing partner, Alta Hayworth, during a masked Halloween ball in downtown Muncie. *Courtesy of the* Muncie Morning Star.

At McGalliard's two-week trial, defense attorneys would suggest a mystery assailant had fired the fatal shot, although they acknowledged their client had pulled a handgun and pointed it at the victim.

Prosecutors said the motive was anger and jealousy, alleging that, that evening, Alta Hayworth had refused to go home with McGalliard.

The defendant, a house painter who lived in Whitely, would testify that he had no memory of the events at the dance after consuming whiskey in a bathroom there.

Asked at a pre-trial hearing if he was guilty, McGalliard responded, "I don't know anything about that, not anything at all."

The jury deliberated for thirty-eight hours over three days before finding McGalliard guilty of second-degree murder and sentencing him to life in prison.

News accounts described the loyalty and support McGalliard's father, then sixty-five, provided his son in the wake of the slaying, visiting him in jail, sitting at the defense table during the trial and standing alongside the defendant when the life sentence was imposed.

Charles McGalliard Sr. would lead efforts to win his son's release, testifying at a 1916 parole board hearing that he believed Alta Hayworth had been shot by another woman, who later committed suicide.

The elder McGalliard lived to see his son pardoned, after more than a dozen years in the state prison, in 1924.

Charles McGalliard Jr.—with the exception of a 1928 alcohol-related arrest in New Castle that led to a brief return to prison—apparently lived out a quiet life in Muncie. He was sixty-one when he died in 1946.

9

JUSTICE DELAYED AND JUSTICE DENIED?

The tragic death of Helen Nokes, beaten to death outside her apartment building in March 1961, was the first event in nearly a decade of uncertainty and frustration for not only authorities prosecuting the case but also for the suspects charged and jailed but not quickly done with the justice system—including a man whose death more than thirty years later would put him in the headlines all over again.

Nokes, a fifty-nine-year-old single woman, was walking home after dark on March 17, 1961. She had been working in a downtown Muncie shop but was on her way back to the Jackson-Vine Apartments when someone attacked her.

When another tenant in the apartment building noticed Nokes hadn't arrived home more than a half hour after the shop closed, she became worried. The friend went outside and found Nokes lying on the sidewalk only a few feet from the door to the building.

Police questioned dozens of people in the neighborhood that night and, thanks to a neighbor looking in a trash can two blocks away, found not only Nokes's purse but also the murder weapon: a rusty iron pipe about eighteen inches long.

Nokes was alive but unconscious when she was found and was rushed first to Muncie's Ball Memorial Hospital and then to an Indianapolis hospital for surgery. But the wounds to her head—so severe that investigators couldn't even tell at first how many times she had been bludgeoned—proved fatal before the ambulance arrived at the hospital.

"A Muncie doctor who examined the woman before she was taken to Indianapolis said the attack was so savage and vicious that the assailant must have intended to kill her. He said she was hit 'too many times and too hard' for it to have been simple robbery," according to a newspaper account.

The length of pipe was so rusty and pitted that police couldn't pull any fingerprints off the murder weapon. But neighbors quickly told police about a man they saw outside in the rain and darkness.

A suspect was found at a nearby restaurant and taken in for questioning; blood was found on his shirt and coat. But the man told police he

Murder defendant Fred Cooper Jr. in April 1962. *Courtesy of Muncie Newspapers Inc.*

had earlier cut himself shaving, and testing determined that he and Nokes shared the same blood type.

Police quickly settled on a trio of suspects. While Nokes was white, the three suspects were African American: Raymond Taylor, Fred Cooper and JoAnne Graham.

Muncie police officials quickly assigned two of their best detectives to the case. Melvin Miller and Ambrose Settles, both pioneering African American investigators, were well known in Muncie's black community.

Thanks to questioning from Miller and Settles, a picture of the murder began to develop, and the early stages of the investigation focused on Taylor, a construction worker described as a "rough character" who had been charged but not prosecuted in connection with the armed robbery of a grocery store in 1959. He had also been held in jail in recent years after threatening to kill a man.

Graham, the woman who had been arrested, told police that she, Taylor and Cooper were driving along Vine Street when Taylor spotted Nokes and said, "I'm going to see what that woman's got." At Taylor's direction, Cooper parked the car in a nearby alley to wait.

"What are you going to do?" Cooper called to Taylor. Then, Graham said, they watched as Taylor approached, confronted and struck Nokes.

"What is wrong with him?" Cooper asked Graham about Taylor. "Is he crazy or something?"

Cooper told police a similar story to the one recounted by Graham but, at the last minute, refused to sign the statement he had made.

Graham and another woman—not named in early newspaper accounts—on hand that night were released from jail, but Taylor and Cooper were held.

After an April 10 court appearance, Cooper told a newspaper reporter, "I'll tell you what it is. It's a ------- frame-up, that's what it is."

A Delaware County grand jury in mid-May indicted Taylor, Cooper and Graham, charging them all with first-degree murder. In the weeks since the killing, Graham had recanted the detailed story she told police shortly after Nokes's murder.

The following month, the shadows cast by the case grew longer.

In late June, police arrested Rainy (Rico) Taylor, the younger brother of defendant Raymond Taylor. While Raymond Taylor was held in jail, his brother went to the home of the until-that-point-unnamed other female witness to the attack.

Rico Taylor kicked in the woman's door and threatened her with a ten-inch butcher knife, police investigator Miller said. The woman drove the younger Taylor away by throwing a chair at him.

Miller said the attack was only the latest in a series of threats, made by several people and aimed at the witness.

By August, two of the defendants were fighting back in the courtroom.

Indianapolis lawyers hired by Cooper and Graham argued that their clients' constitutional rights had been violated. They had not been advised of those rights, the lawyers argued, and local newspaper reporters had urged the two to cooperate with police.

By this time, an article appeared in a national magazine, *Master Detective*, giving details of the case. The lawyers also argued that the magazine had prejudiced potential jurors against the defendants.

The case had been moved from Muncie and Delaware County to Winchester in neighboring Randolph County after defense attorneys argued their clients couldn't get a fair trial in Muncie.

As 1961 turned into 1962, however, the defendants still hadn't gone to trial. It was the first delay in administering justice in Helen Nokes's slaying.

An initial round of trials in the spring of 1962 saw Graham acquitted and a jury fail to reach a verdict on Cooper and Taylor.

Attorneys and prosecutors in the April 1962 murder trial of Fred Cooper Jr. confer with Judge John W. Macy. *Courtesy of Muncie Newspapers Inc.*

New charges were filed as Cooper and Taylor remained in jail. Months turned into years, and Taylor, by that time thirty, and Cooper, now twenty-six, didn't go to trial again until the spring of 1964. When they did see a courtroom, the men were not charged with murder.

Taylor was found guilty of robbery and inflicting physical injury during a robbery. The first charge carried a sentence of up to twenty-five years and the second, a sentence of life in prison.

For his role in driving the car the night Nokes was robbed and killed, Cooper was charged with robbery.

Much of the delay centered on the statement—sometimes referred to as a confession—given by Cooper that he later refused to sign.

"Cooper alleges [the statement] was beaten out of him" by Miller and Settles, according to newspaper accounts.

Ultimately, the trial of Cooper and Taylor would take eight weeks. When it was all over, Taylor was sentenced to life plus ten to twenty-five years. Cooper was sentenced to ten to twenty-five years. Cooper was sent to the

Delaware County deputy prosecutor James J. Jordan holds slaying victim
Helen Nokes's purse during Fred Cooper Jr.'s April 1962 murder trial.
Courtesy of Muncie Newspapers Inc.

Indiana Reformatory in Pendleton, and Taylor was sent to the Indiana State
Prison in Michigan City.

That didn't stick, however.

In December 1967, more than six years after Helen Nokes was killed, the
Indiana Supreme Court reversed the convictions of Cooper and Taylor.

The high court's reversal was centered on the butcher knife that Taylor's
brother, Rico, allegedly used to intimidate a witness.

"Rico Taylor admitted he had previously pleaded guilty in a different assault and battery case involving a state's witness and the trial court let the knife be introduced in evidence," the *Muncie Star* reported on December 13, 1967. "But the Supreme Court held that with no proof the knife was used, Rico Taylor's testimony was not impeached." The knife was not relevant to the trial, the high court said, but was allowed into evidence anyway.

With the likelihood of new trials on the horizon following the Supreme Court's reversal, Delaware County prosecutor Robert Robinson became the third prosecutor to take on the case.

But Robinson acknowledged, in the summer of 1968, the near impossibility of mounting new trials seven years after Helen Nokes's murder. Since the 1964 trial, two witnesses in the case had died, and several others could no longer be located.

In May 1968, Robinson dismissed the robbery charge against Fred Cooper. Wearing "a neat blue suit," Cooper was released from custody and walked, smiling, from the courtroom.

In June 1968, Taylor also walked out of a courtroom a free man after serving seven years in jail.

The cost of the case also weighed heavily on the minds of court officials over the years.

"Every slow turn of the wheels of justice in the Nokes robbery case…means additional expense to the taxpayers," began one newspaper article during the 1964 trial.

The article noted that jurors were paid $7.50 a day plus ten cents for each mile of travel to the out-of-county trial. "Meals are also provided," the article noted.

"The breakdown of the cost to try the case at Winchester looks like this: Lodging for prisoners, $802.20; jurors, $2,760.80; jury commissioners, $10; court bailiff, $65; court reporter, $104; heat, light and power, $30; telephone, $12.55; county clerk, $72; and per diem of judge, $140."

If anyone thought it was unusual that utilities to keep the courthouse well lit and warm—in the summer months, no less—would be so scrupulously tracked, the record suggests they didn't speak up.

In July 1964—four years before the cases against Cooper and Taylor were dropped—a terse newspaper article noted that the cost to Delaware County so far was $40,000.

"Both defendants…have indicated they wish to appeal their case, which would add to the expense that must be paid by Delaware County," the four-paragraph article noted.

It would be another four years before Taylor and Cooper, the latter having always claimed only to be driving the car the night Helen Nokes was killed, would be free and twenty-seven years before Cooper once again made headlines in Muncie.

On May 30, 1995, fire broke out in an eastside Muncie home. The blaze destroyed the structure and killed the man who lived there: Fred Cooper, by that point a senior citizen.

Food left unattended on a stove started the blaze, fire investigators said.

Cooper's sister said her brother, during his seven years in jail, had earned thirteen certificates in skills such as barbering, leather making and shoe repair.

But after he was released, Cooper's fortunes did not significantly improve. He married but quickly divorced, his sister said. Although Cooper stayed employed, she added, he became an alcoholic.

"Prison took his life," his sister said. The fire only ended his existence.

MUNCIE'S HOUSES OF ILL FAME

In some quarters, just whispering Babe Swartz's name was enough to make men tremble.

Arrested for prostitution more times than perhaps any other woman in Delaware County history, Swartz was a notorious figure in the 1960s and '70s. She operated a truck stop that was legendary and kept a little black book of customers' names that was even more legendary.

And then she ran for the highest law enforcement office in the county.

Viola Christina Swartz's life began modestly in the town of Bedford, Indiana. She went to school in Bedford and, as her 2001 obituary noted, was a homemaker and attended church.

Sometime between her early years in southern Indiana and 1967, Swartz moved to Muncie, and the saga of her battle with law enforcement began.

In November 1967, five Delaware County sheriff's deputies and five Indiana State Police troopers raided the truck stop that bore Swartz's nickname. Babe's Truck Stop, located along Indiana 28 north of Muncie, had been under surveillance by police, who believed prostitutes were working out of five rooms, or apartments, behind the truck stop.

Although Babe Swartz was on police radar, she was less well known to the public at large and, apparently, to newspaper reporters. The first story about the raid called her Violet C. "Babe" Swartz rather than Viola.

But Muncie's fascination with and determination to stamp out prostitution predated the raid on Babe's by decades.

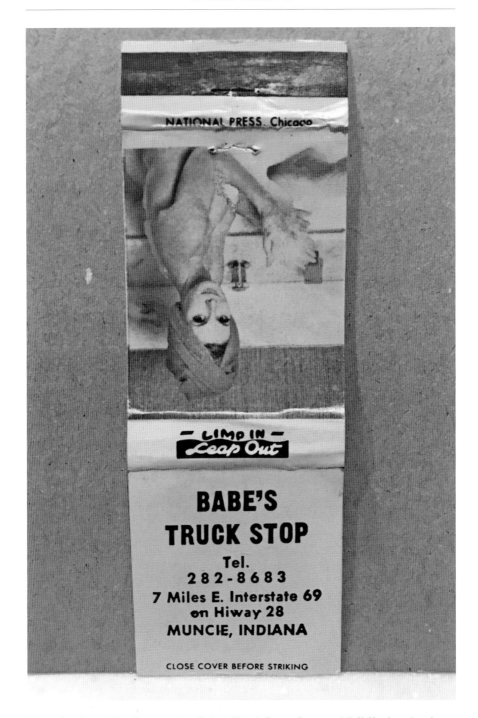

An undated matchbook promoting Babe's Truck Stop. *Courtesy of Jeff Koenker, photo by Keith Roysdon.*

A Ball State University sociologist, Anne Szopa, studied prostitution in Muncie from 1890 to 1920. In the 1920s, Muncie was the subject of the famous "Middletown" studies that painted the city—anonymously—as America's typical small city.

Szopa said in a 1989 interview that studying prostitution in the city's boom years, from the late 1800s to the early 1920s, offered an interesting look at how the city changed.

"In the 1890s, no one was really concerned about prostitution," Szopa told the *Muncie Evening Press* in 1989. It was tolerated. "There were some routine arrests, but no organized efforts to condemn or eliminate prostitution.

"By 1904, several social reform groups were crusading to limit alcohol sales, gambling houses and notorious taverns," she said. "Prostitutes and alcohol were linked together as social evils, and the image of the prostitute became that of a foul, depraved hag."

Prohibitionists in the years before national Prohibition depicted prostitution as an alcohol-fueled evil, she said.

When ordinances around the turn of the century restricted taverns to certain areas of town, those spots turned into red-light districts where prostitution thrived.

Sometimes prostitutes were seen as victims to be rescued, particularly by the community's "upstanding" women. But such efforts were not successful, and prostitution continued in Muncie.

Law enforcement's take on prostitution was much like its take on gambling: police it and try to stamp it out. That attitude continued into the late twentieth century, with raids on "massage parlors" and brothels.

In 1972, police arrested a woman for keeping a house of prostitution. News accounts noted that she was eighty-five years old and in a wheelchair. The woman's house was raided after "anonymous complaints about what goes on there," according to one newspaper account.

And then there was Babe Swartz.

Around dinnertime on November 15, 1967, while diners ate in the truck stop's restaurant, those ten officers pushed their way into the apartments behind Babe's Truck Stop and arrested Swartz and three women. The women were charged with prostitution. Two men were arrested for "visiting a house of ill fame." Swartz was charged with "operating a house of ill fame."

Photos in the *Muncie Star* show investigators counting $427 from the cash box and questioning the women who worked in the truck stop's apartments.

The names of the restaurant's patrons were recorded by officers.

An undated pocketknife promoting Babe's Truck Stop. *Courtesy of Jeff Koenker, photo by Keith Roysdon.*

By the second day of coverage, newspaper stories correctly identified Viola "Babe" Swartz. Her name would continue to make headlines for years to come.

Swartz and the women posted bonds—$250 compared to $100 for the men—and business at Babe's continued. In May 1968, another police raid resulted in the arrests of six women, including Swartz.

As those cases dragged on in court, the Delaware County prosecutor's office sought a court order in 1969 to literally shut the doors at Babe's. Prosecutor Robert Robinson not only wanted the building padlocked but also sought an injunction asking that the furniture and fixtures be held and not removed. Robinson wanted no activity at the truck stop for a year.

Robinson argued that Babe's was used for "the purpose of lewdness, assignation and prostitution."

Authorities wanted a permanent end to activities at Babe's and wanted to sell the furniture and equipment.

The efforts failed, however, and Babe's stayed in business—and stayed in the crosshairs of police and prosecutors.

Raids continued and charges continued, including—in July 1971—an allegation that Swartz not only conducted prostitution activities and possessed illegal drugs but also committed "illegal possession of fireworks."

The big development in local law enforcement's war against Swartz came in June 1972, when she was charged with bribery.

Court documents alleged that Swartz gave Prosecutor David Casterline $500 "to avoid prosecution of charges." Casterline gave the money to state police, who began an investigation that lasted several weeks.

Swartz was read the arrest warrant by state police officers and taken into custody but "released on her own recognizance"—in other words, without paying bail—"two minutes after arriving at the Delaware County Jail," according to a newspaper account.

Swartz wasn't alone in facing bribery charges that week. A few days earlier, Sheriff James P. Carey had been charged along with three other men, including the owner of a popular bar, the owner of a vending machine company and the owner of a cigar store.

Officials soon applied more pressure on Babe's Truck Stop. In July 1972, authorities wrote to the gas company, telephone company and electric company to get them to shut off utilities.

A gas company spokesman noted that the Indiana Utility Regulatory Commission was unlikely to allow cutting off service if the customer was paying bills and not using the utility to create a "dangerous situation or public hazard."

And when the telephone company did agree to shut off service, circuit court judge Alva Cox issued an order restraining the company from doing so.

In the meantime, the raids continued. In October 1972, county police again raided Babe's and arrested Swartz and several others.

A county police captain acknowledged that, despite seven raids he had participated in over the past five years, no cases stemming from the Babe's raids had come to trial.

"Why? I can't say. I can say the letdown is beyond our department. The sheriff has always told us if there is prostitution or vice and you've got a good case, raid it."

By this point, Swartz was forty-eight years old and had been targeted for several years. But the cases always fell short.

By October 1972, the prosecutor's efforts to "padlock" Babe's and shut the truck stop down had been delayed and delayed. A court hearing on the request was postponed a sixth time that month.

Rumors had always circulated that Swartz had a little black book, a secret list of the men who visited her truck stop. On that list, rumors indicated, were the names of powerful local men.

In November 1972, the *Muncie Star* reported that Swartz's trial on the bribery charge had been postponed.

"No new date was set for the trial, which apparently was rescheduled, because the prosecutor's office was unaware that it was set to begin with," the newspaper reported.

As the wheels of justice ground slowly, things changed for Swartz and her truck stop.

Police raids continued in June 1973, but newspaper accounts noted that the truck stop's name had been changed from Babe's to Sebab's, a simple switch of the sequence of letters.

By September 1973, newspaper articles were referring to Swartz as the former owner of the truck stop. Swartz was not among those charged in later raids.

In February 1974, a one-paragraph story noted that a local bank had foreclosed on the truck stop. Considering all the notoriety and headlines over the years, the two-sentence story seemed oddly brief.

Viola "Babe" Swartz. *Courtesy of Muncie Newspapers Inc.*

Then, one month later, in March 1974, Swartz generated a newspaper headline—but not, this time, for being arrested.

"'Babe' Swartz Enters Sheriff Race on Democrat Ticket against Carey," the headline read.

The fifty-year-old Swartz became the sixth candidate to file to run in the 1974 sheriff's primary election.

"She ran the truck stop on Ind. 28 northwest of Muncie for 13 years," the article noted. "During which she said she was arrested 'about 39 times' on various charges, most of them relating to prostitution. She never has been convicted."

For the past ten months, Babe Swartz had been working as a waitress at the Way II Tavern, owned by Randall S. "Front Porch" Harmon, a former one-term U.S. congressman who was notorious in 1958 for renting his front porch to the government as his congressional district office.

"I'm running because everyone wanted me to," Swartz said about the sheriff's election. That included Harmon, who co-owned the Way II Tavern with Swartz's son, she said.

If elected, Swartz said, she would "stop this harassment by police on people like myself."

She also wanted to "get rid of the system of payoffs to police."

"I need all the moral support people can give me."

When contacted for comment on Swartz's candidacy, Sheriff Carey—whose department had targeted Swartz dozens of times—said, "It's a free world."

In the end, Swartz didn't pose much of a threat to Carey, who won the primary election with 53 percent, or 6,886 votes. Swartz won 625 votes and finished fourth in the crowded field.

During the months leading up to the election, rumors flew that Swartz might release the names in her little black book. The public speculated about the names. Would top lawmen, attorneys or elected officials be included?

But the names in Babe's book, if it even existed, were never made public.

Less than a year after the election, the final chapter for Babe's truck stop was written.

Fire swept through the truck stop in March 1975. Flames were shooting fifteen feet above the roof of the building when firefighters arrived. The building had been vacant at the time of the fire.

A few months later, Swartz—who had, during her election campaign, noted that she had been arrested thirty-nine times but never convicted—finally faced a tough judgment.

Swartz was charged in federal court with tax evasion, and in September 1975, she was sentenced to a year in prison.

U.S. District Court judge S. Hugh Dillin said Swartz's seemingly bulletproof history "was some indication of the judicial system in Delaware County."

After the resolution of her tax evasion case, Viola Christina "Babe" Swartz lived her remaining years out of the headlines. She died in November 2001.

If Babe Swartz had secrets to tell, she took them with her to the grave.

Who Killed Norman Black?

The 1910 murder—some called it an assassination—of Muncie businessman Norman E. Black provided one of the great local mysteries of the early twentieth century.

The Black slaying—or, more specifically, the events that followed it—also served to tarnish the city's image on a statewide basis.

In the early evening of Thursday, September 22, 1910, the sixty-two-year-old Black picked up his horse and buggy at the Bud Thomas livery barn, as was his nightly custom. About forty-five minutes later, the horse and buggy returned to the barn, near Mulberry and Howard Streets. Employees were at first startled to notice the horse had returned of its own accord and then realized that Black, his head and body covered with a riding blanket, was slumped in a corner of the carriage.

Closer inspection revealed that Black was unconscious and suffering from a gunshot wound in the right side of his head. His hat, on the seat beside him, had what appeared to be a bullet hole. The blanket was saturated with blood and brain matter.

The mortally wounded Black was taken first to a nearby physician's office and then to the Mix hospital, on the second floor of a downtown office building.

His wife and children were alerted, and a death watch began. Friends—some from Black's hometown of Selma, where he, for a time, owned most of the business district—gathered outside the hospital and could hear the dying man's moans. He succumbed to the gunshot wound later that night.

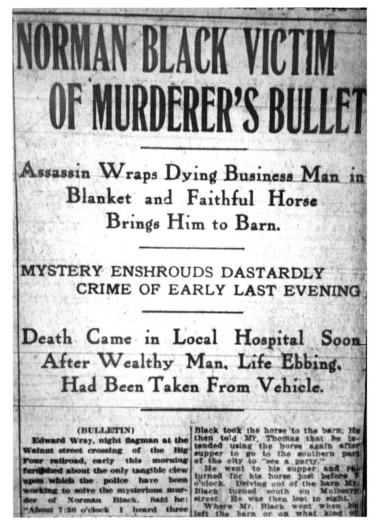

NORMAN BLACK VICTIM OF MURDERER'S BULLET

Assassin Wraps Dying Business Man in Blanket and Faithful Horse Brings Him to Barn.

MYSTERY ENSHROUDS DASTARDLY CRIME OF EARLY LAST EVENING

Death Came in Local Hospital Soon After Wealthy Man, Life Ebbing, Had Been Taken From Vehicle.

(BULLETIN)

Edward Wray, night flagman at the Walnut street crossing of the Big Four railroad, early this morning furnished about the only tangible clew upon which the police have been working to solve the mysterious murder of Norman Black. Said he: "About 7:30 o'clock I heard three

Black took the horse to the barn. He then told Mr. Thomas that he intended using the horse again after supper to go to the southern part of the city to "see a party."

He went to his supper and returned for his horse just before 8 o'clock. Driving out of the barn Mr. Black turned south on Mulberry street. He was then lost to sight. Where Mr. Black went when he left the barn or on what kind of

The mysterious slaying of businessman Norman Black made headlines not only in Muncie but also throughout the Midwest. *Courtesy of the* Muncie Morning Star.

Black was perhaps best known as vice-president of the Peoples National Bank and had remained on its board after it became a trust company. At the time of his death, he owned two business blocks in downtown Muncie, along with several area farms and other properties.

Initial speculation was that Black—who routinely wore a diamond ring worth $400—had been the target of a bandit. The ring was later found in his safe deposit box, however.

The day after the slaying, members of the Muncie Police Board announced their "firm belief" that a reward of at least $1,000 would be offered in the case.

Delaware County commissioner Enoch Drumm said he was "strongly in favor" of the county offering a reward.

"Delaware County and Muncie should not allow [the killer] to escape if mere money will bring him to justice," Drumm told the *Muncie Morning Star*.

Mayor Edward Tuhey, meanwhile, announced he was taking "personal charge" of the investigation, declaring that every available officer would be involved in the search for the killer.

The night after the slaying, two police officers boarded

Mayor Edward Tuhey announced he was taking charge of the Black murder investigation. Later, he fought efforts to offer a reward for information on the crime. *Courtesy of Muncie Newspapers Inc.*

Black's buggy and let his horse take them where it may. According to some accounts, it traveled to a home in southwest Muncie, stopped briefly and then returned to the livery barn.

Muncie police chief Otto Williamson scoffed at suggestions that the horse's travels meant anything. The mystery—and the role the horse played in it—drew national attention, however.

"Wisdom of Old Horse May Revenge Murder," a headline in the *Topeka Daily Capital* read.

Then the investigation took a turn that appeared to make local authorities uneasy.

Several witnesses came forward to say that Black, as many as six nights a week, drove his carriage to a former iron factory at Second and Franklin Streets, where he would pick up a woman waiting there and drive on to points unknown.

While it was never officially determined, authorities came to believe that Black was most likely shot in the area of Second and Mulberry Streets.

A resident said she saw a woman standing near a carriage at that intersection about the time the shot was believed to have been fired.

And a grocer, whose store was about one block away on Walnut Street, reported a woman, appearing frightened, had hurried past his business with blood visible on her "light linen suit." Media accounts began referring to her as "the woman in white."

When the next week came, the county commissioners and Muncie City Council took no steps to fund a reward. Mayor Tuhey publicly opposed posting a reward, saying he wanted to give his officers more time to unravel the mystery.

Within a day of the slaying, the *Muncie Evening Press* reported it was known "that members of the Black family would be pleased if the investigations could not uncover the purpose of Black's visit to the south side." The newspaper also noted that "gossipers" were suggesting city police "were not trying to capture the murderer."

Chief Williamson took exception to such suggestions. "We'll capture the murderer of Norman Black if it takes six years," he proclaimed.

(Within two weeks after the slaying, Williamson had other concerns. He was arrested on allegations that he held a business interest in a cigar store that doubled as a gambling parlor at the same time city police had raided similar—and presumably competing—gambling operations. The following February, the chief was convicted of a related misdemeanor charge, drawing a ten-dollar fine.)

After early reports that an arrest was imminent in the Black killing—and a Selma woman was questioned by police for up to four hours—the case appeared to quickly go cold.

County coroner Aaron Cecil didn't conduct an inquiry into the death until early October and seemed to only reach a conclusion that Black had been a victim of foul play.

The *Evening Press* criticized the coroner for waiting nearly two

Mystery of Murder Is Unsolved

Local authorities seemed to quickly lose interest in solving the September 1910 slaying of Muncie businessman Norman Black. *Courtesy of the* Muncie Morning Star.

weeks to hold his hearing. "With his customary slowness, [Cecil] has proceeded falteringly in his one-week-behind-the-times investigation," it wrote.

With the case seemingly going nowhere, a Delaware County grand jury launched an investigation that December—apparently to the surprise of Prosecutor Harry Long.

One week later, the grand jurors said they had not uncovered evidence that would justify an indictment but publicly urged the commissioners to offer a "suitable reward."

Witnesses before the grand jury had included at least three local women—all married—and the victim's son, Edgar Claire Black. He was asked, perhaps, about reports that some of his father's personal papers had been destroyed before they could be reviewed by police.

The grand jury's suggestion aside, neither city nor county officials took any steps toward offering a reward without explaining why that was the case. The mystery fairly quickly faded from local headlines.

In March 1911, the *Indianapolis News* sent a reporter to Muncie to investigate Black's murder.

He concluded that "big business and politics have interfered to make the assassin's safety secure."

Black was "a man of many gallantries, and his escapades, if made public, would expose men identified with business and politics," he wrote.

"After a brief flurry, the investigation stopped. Every effort was made to hush the matter up. …No one here believes that the man who took Norman E. Black's life will ever be brought to justice."

The next month, the *Hartford City News* weighed in.

"Muncie has time and time again proved that it is a very peculiar community," it reported.

> *Where else outside of some Chinese or Russian province could a murderer run at large without fear of punishment?*
>
> [Black's killer] *is rich and influential, with powerful connections. And Muncie claims to be a highly civilized community.*

The man to whom the out-of-town publications were referring was never publicly identified, and he—or anyone else—never faced charges stemming from Black's death.

PINBALL TO SLOT MACHINES

Muncie "Cracks Down" on Gambling

Throughout much of the twentieth century, Muncie had a love-hate relationship with illegal gambling.

Gambling of any kind—card games, slot machines, even pinball—fell under the scrutiny of Muncie's law enforcement agencies in the 1950s, '60s and '70s.

Raids were conducted, gambling devices were seized and sometimes destroyed and charges were filed. And then, often, those charges were dropped.

The story of gambling in Muncie might have reached its peak in February 1972, when, after a police raid on a cigar store where gambling took place in a back room, a judge came to the store and conducted court proceedings rather than move the many defendants and large amount of evidence to a courtroom.

Muncie and all of Indiana has been conflicted about gambling. In 1953, the state legislature passed the Hasbrook anti-gambling law, which outlawed all forms of gambling—unless they were conducted by religious, patriotic or fraternal groups.

That exemption didn't last long. On June 30, 1953, the *Chicago Tribune* reported that the Indiana Supreme Court ruled that the Hasbrook law violated the state constitution because it allowed gambling by certain groups.

The *Tribune* story noted that the high court's ruling did not have an impact on Indiana's other gambling laws. Slot machines and other forms of gambling were still illegal.

Nine years later, oddly enough, the Hasbrook anti-gambling law was still being cited by police and prosecutors as they cracked down on—pinball machines.

In March 1964, Delaware County prosecutor Hugh Tuck Schulhof and his deputies, John Stern and Charles "Chic" Clark, said that most pinball machines in the county were illegal.

"If there is a mechanism that gives a free game upon attainment of a certain score, then that would be legal," Schulhof told the *Muncie Evening Press* in a March 21, 1964 article. "Our position is that any more than one free game awarded by the machine at the time a game is being played would necessitate a 'recording device,'" a necessary step toward gambling on the machines.

Police said pinball machines

Piece Work

Police Chief Cordell Campbell smashed Tuesday a Lucky Seven gambling device confiscated at the Amvets club, 3421 S. Walnut St., May 16, 1973. Last month Judge Pro-Tem Larry Helm ordered the machine destroyed and the money in it turned over to the PAL Club. Several other gambling devices are being held by the police department pending court action. Assisting in the destruction of the machine is police officer Tom Curtis. (Star Photo)

Muncie Police chief Cordell Campbell destroying a seized gambling machine. *Courtesy of Muncie Newspapers Inc.*

were present in nine locations around the city, and the prosecutor said another two dozen machines might be scattered in rural areas.

The number appeared to be down substantially from 1959, when as many as six hundred machines were placed around the county. All of them were owned by thirteen people, the newspaper said.

A Muncie man had even been convicted of possession of a gambling device in 1959. He was fined fifty dollars.

By 1964, one machine could make as much as forty dollars in a weekend, which was split between the machine's owner and the proprietor of the establishment where it was located.

The prosecutor gave businesses until April 1 to remove the machines. In mid-April, newspapers reported, machines had been removed, including one at an Eaton service station that was removed the same day Schulhof heard about it.

The upset over pinball machines was motivated in part because the community's youngsters were using them.

"Schulhof said he has had a complaint from a Selma minister who said school children were spending their lunch money in the 'no-arm bandits,'" the newspaper reported.

In Muncie, gamblers started young.

> *According to a complaint, prizes were offered to entice youngsters to "play" penny bubblegum machines. If the purchaser received a certain color ball of bubble gum, bonus bubble gum was given. Another pre-designated color resulted in a small cash prize, the sheriff was told.*

The bubble gum machine was removed from its location.

While the 1964 World Series, which pitted the St. Louis Cardinals against the New York Yankees, was underway, police arrested a sixty-nine-year-old man accused of charging a juvenile a fee to play a "World Series" pinball machine.

By 1971, the community's love-hate relationship with gambling was in full flower.

Then-prosecutor David Casterline—leading a group of police officers called "Casterline's Raiders" in an April 24, 1971 *Muncie Star* headline—charged into a local Veterans of Foreign Wars hall and found four slot machines and six thousand "tip books" (paper gambling devices somewhat like modern-day scratch-off lottery tickets) in a secret room used for gambling.

"Authorities said the back room had a swinging wall set on coasters that opened and shut automatically," the newspaper reported. "One officer said part of the room construction gives the impression that one is walking through a trophy case in order to get to where the gambling apparatus was being operated."

"I feel constitutionally bound to stop gambling in Delaware County," the prosecutor said.

Raids against Muncie gambling continued. A few months later, police raided a craps game in an alley on the city's northeast side. They discovered, besides several people who stuffed money in their pockets when they saw police coming, an old couch, chairs and a table.

Citing the furniture as a fire hazard, officers poured a bottle of wine one of the offenders had been drinking onto the davenport and called fireman Joe Greer to bring a can of gasoline from the fire station across the street. The gasoline was poured onto the furniture, which was stacked into a pile. As the men and fireman Greer watched, the furniture was then set ablaze by police.

In October 1971, "a small army" of state troopers raided six locations around the city and arrested fifty people for gambling. Raids were conducted at private homes, as well as in locations like the Glamour Inn and the Greenpoint Tavern.

George Nixon, a candidate for mayor, complained that Muncie police were not involved in the widespread raids. Police chief Cordell Campbell replied that "certainly gambling and other vice is a part of our law enforcement, but our main concern is to make the streets and homes in Muncie safe."

But within a day or two, Campbell authorized another raid, at the Top Hat Cigar Store downtown, that led to the arrest of twenty people. Along with money, "several hundred" packs of playing cards were seized, as well as three .38-caliber handguns.

A few days later, city police raided Pete's Cigar and Lunch on South Walnut Street, arresting fifteen people on gambling charges after officers in civilian clothes watched the illegal sale of tip books.

Police chief Campbell was optimistic.

"I feel good about the whole thing," Campbell was quoted as saying in an October 15, 1971 article in the *Muncie Star*. "I'm sure this town will soon be rid of vice—all vice."

The good feeling didn't last long. Later, in October 1971, Prosecutor Casterline dropped charges against the men arrested at the Top Hat Cigar Store.

Casterline said police did not contact his office before the raid, and no warrant had been issued, meaning the seizure of evidence was unlawful.

Campbell expressed frustration.

"I'm not an attorney," he said. "But all the training I've had, including the FBI Academy, would indicate that we had cause to believe there was gambling going on inside the store. We're duty bound to enforce the law."

Another visit to the Top Hat, in February 1972, is the raid that prompted city court judge Joseph Rankin to bring court to the store for the processing of the two dozen people arrested.

One month later, Rankin dismissed the charges and ordered city police to return the gambling equipment seized, and defense attorney John Brumfield called the raids "harassment."

But police raids continued, including one, in November 1972, against a local American Legion post, where two gambling machines were seized. Gamblers fed twenty-five cents into the machines, which looked like gumball machines. They received plastic capsules with "tip" sheets inside. Prizes of up to ten dollars were supposedly awarded for tips that ended in sevens or double sevens.

"We have moved forward in our efforts to battle syndicate crime," Campbell said. "We do know there is organized crime watching Muncie and searching for an opening. We are going to make certain the door is never left open."

Throughout 1972 and into 1973, raids continued at fraternal halls, labor halls, taverns and cigar stores, including the Top Hat.

Sometimes the raids were even more of an embarrassment than others.

A September 1972 raid on a Moose lodge was expected to lead to charges against a longtime Muncie police officer who was a lodge officer. And the city's traffic director was charged in May 1973 because he was an officer of an Amvets post that was raided.

Police often demolished seized gambling machines, but in October 1982, Delaware County Court judge Betty Shelton Cole told one man he could have his seized "penny drop" machines back if he donated $2,000 to a fund to replace the county children's home.

No newspaper articles indicate whether he took the judge up on the deal.

The "Happy Anniversary" Murder

From the beginning, authorities were skeptical about thirty-year-old Loyed Chandler Key's account of how his wife ended up dead in their car along Interstate 69 in southwestern Delaware County.

Shortly after midnight on Sunday, March 21, 1965, a seemingly frantic Key—his car off the northbound lanes of the interstate, about 1.7 miles north of the Daleville exit—had waved down a passing motorist and told him to get help.

That man, in turn, had climbed a fence and run to a nearby farmhouse, where he called state police. Key—an Alabama native who lived in Muncie from 1960 until 1963, when his family relocated to Marion—said he and his twenty-nine-year-old wife, Ethel, had been returning home from Greenfield when his vehicle was pulled over in Delaware County by a vehicle with a "flashing red light."

Key said he assumed he was being stopped by a police officer but was instead confronted by two gun-toting black males, who took his wallet, containing about $200, before forcing him to lie on the pavement under his car.

While under the car, Key said, he heard several gunshots before the assailants ran back to their car, drove across the interstate's median and fled down its southbound lanes.

The Marion man said he then found his wife—the mother of their four children, ranging in age from three to twelve—mortally wounded in the front seat of their car. Her purse was missing.

Ex-Muncie resident Loyed Key sits with his lawyer on the day Key pleaded guilty to murdering his wife, Ethel, as the couple traveled on I-69 after renewing their wedding vows. *Courtesy of Muncie Newspapers Inc.*

A state trooper reported the victim was "sitting upright" on the car seat, covered in blood, but there were no indications a struggle had taken place.

A pathologist would later testify that Ethel had likely died instantly when she was shot six times, once in the back of her head and five times in the left temple.

The final day of her life had been a festive one for Ethel Key.

Four days short of thirteen years earlier, the former Ethel Grace had been sixteen when she and her seventeen-year-old boyfriend were married by a justice of the peace in their native Alabama.

That Saturday, at Loyed's instigation, they made the sixty-mile trip to Greenfield, where they stood before a pastor they had known in Muncie, E. Jack Gambill, as they renewed their wedding vows.

After hearing of the tragedy that had unfolded on the couple's trip home, Gambill declared the Keys had been "very much in love."

The Keys had behaved "almost as if they were newly married," the minister's wife added.

Those attending a Greenfield revival service that preceded the renewal of the couple's vows would later recall that Loyed Key had persuaded his wife to step to the front of the congregation and pray, although he did not join her there.

"She was a good Christian woman and was in a state of grace," Pastor Gambill said. "Perhaps we can take some consolation in that."

Loyed Key was eventually taken to a state police facility for a polygraph exam, but its operators told investigators he was too exhausted to be tested.

The widower assured state police and Delaware County sheriff's deputies that he would submit to the lie detector test in a few days, after returning with his children from Alabama, where his wife would be buried on their thirteenth wedding anniversary.

Before Loyed Key returned to Indiana, however, police had cracked the murder case.

A Madison County man reported to deputies that his cousin, Phyllis Jean Hazelbaker—a divorced mother of three children who lived in Alexandria—had offered him $200 to travel to Muncie and corroborate Loyed Key's account of a car with flashing red lights occupied by two black men.

(An account of a similar incident involving bogus police in northwestern Ohio, absent any violence, had appeared in local newspapers a few days before Ethel Key's slaying.)

Police found the thirty-year-old Hazelbaker at her place of employment, the Fisher Guide plant in Anderson.

Questioned on the day of Ethel Key's funeral, Hazelbaker acknowledged being acquainted with Loyed but denied any involvement in his wife's slaying.

After she was informed that a polygraph test indicated she wasn't being truthful, however, Hazelbaker confessed, providing details of her four-year affair with Loyed Key and their conspiracy to kill his wife.

Phyllis Hazelbaker said she met Key at a Marion drive-in restaurant in 1960, the year she was divorced. For the first several months of their relationship, she said, she believed he was an unmarried Muncie resident named Joe Key who worked at the Fisher Body plant in Marion.

At one point, when she hadn't heard from "Joe" for several days, Hazelbaker recalled, she went to his Muncie home—in the 2500 block of West Twenty-seventh Street—and came face to face with his wife.

Ethel called Loyed home that day, Hazelbaker said, and he denied knowing their visitor from Alexandria.

Later, Phyllis said, Loyed castigated her because she had "queered his chance of getting a divorce so they could be married."

Eventually, Hazelbaker told police, they began discussing plans to eliminate Ethel so they could begin a life together. Loyed tried to drown his wife on a fishing trip to Alabama, she said.

In the fall of 1964, Phyllis said, Loyed told her Ethel was seriously ill, had undergone surgery and was believed to have only a few weeks to live. She apparently recovered, however.

At some point, either Loyed or Phyllis went to a Marion veterinarian's clinic and purchased tablets of a powerful barbiturate, purportedly to be used to "put down" an ailing dog.

She said Loyed had intended to use the pills to poison Ethel. Police would find the capsules in the glove box of his car.

There was also discussion of causing a gas heater in the Key home to malfunction and catch on fire.

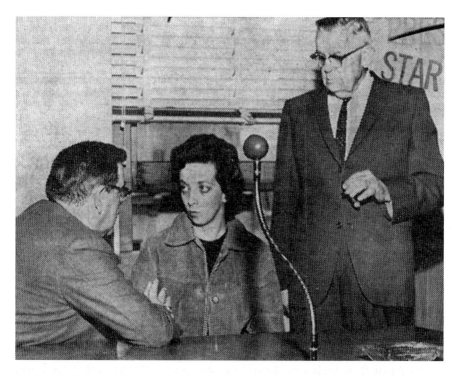

Phyllis Hazelbaker, convicted of plotting with her boyfriend, Loyed Key, to kill his wife, meets with her attorneys. *Courtesy of the Muncie Newspapers Inc.*

Still later, a plan was hatched to shoot Ethel during a staged robbery.

The idea for the Keys to renew their wedding vows for their thirteenth anniversary was designed to throw off any suspicion that Loyed played a role in his wife's death.

On March 20, Phyllis told police, she had followed Loyed's instructions, tailing the Keys on their trip to Greenfield and then on their northbound trip up I-69.

Hazelbaker said when she pulled up behind the Keys' vehicle, stopped along the unlighted interstate north of Daleville, Loyed approached her car; dropped a .32-caliber handgun, his wallet and Ethel's purse onto her lap; and said, "Get going!"

Phyllis said she had also provided Loyed with a washcloth to wipe blood from his hands.

Hazelbaker led authorities to Ethel's purse—thrown along the interstate just south of what later became the Indiana 332 exit—and then to the murder weapon, recovered by state police "skin divers" from the Mississinewa River near Marion.

After reviewing the information provided by Phyllis, Delaware County prosecutor Hugh Tuck Schulhof contacted Alabama State Police and asked them to arrest Loyed Key on a murder charge.

The Alabama troopers determined that Loyed, his four children and his parents had already left for Indiana.

Key was arrested when his traveling party reached Elizabethtown, Kentucky.

Returned to Delaware County, Loyed at first denied Hazelbaker's claims. Later, however, after praying in his jail cell with his father—the elder Key was a pastor and used car salesman in Jasper, Alabama, newspapers reported—Loyed gave police a statement admitting he had killed Ethel.

He also described himself as a victim of domestic violence, saying his wife had left him with fingernail scars and pocketknife wounds.

"I kept it all bottled up in me," he told police. "I just couldn't take it any more."

He said he had retrieved the handgun from under his seat and fired the first shot into the back of Ethel's head while their car was still traveling up the interstate.

Word of a slaying linked to a love triangle quickly drew national attention. The crime became known as the "Happy Anniversary" murder.

"Happy Anniversary, Dear—Bang! Bang! Bang!" read a headline in the *Palm Springs (CA) Desert Sun*.

On April 2, a Delaware County grand jury indicted both Loyed and Hazelbaker on first-degree murder charges.

Veteran Muncie attorney Clarence Benadum, Hazelbaker's public defender, issued a statement on behalf of his client.

"Phyllis Jean Hazelbaker, my client, is a victim of mind-warping, clandestine love, as was King David, who wrote the Psalms," Benadum wrote.

Within days, Loyed Key had changed his account of Ethel's killing, the first of several times he would revise the details of his story. He called Pastor Gambill to the jail from Greenfield to help him prepare a written statement in which he maintained that Phyllis had actually fired the fatal gunshots.

(Loyed said he needed the assistance because he had a third-grade education and could barely read and write. Two of Ethel's sisters lived in Muncie, and one came forward to say Loyed had remained in school at least through the ninth grade and was only pretending to be illiterate.)

"I opened the door [to Phyllis's car] and threw the gun on the seat and said, 'I haven't got the guts,'" Loyed said. "I've been trying to protect the other woman. I didn't do the shooting, but I know I'm just as guilty as she is."

"I didn't step one foot out of my car," was Hazelbaker's response.

"I'm so deeply shocked by this turn of events," Minister Gambill told reporters. "She was very happy, and he seemed happy, too."

After his wife's death, the pastor added, Loyed had "seemed so upset, so sincere."

On April 17, Loyed was reported to be planning an escape from the Delaware County jail with a Milwaukee man awaiting trial on a robbery charge. Both men were placed in "solitary confinement," deputies said.

Four days later, accompanied by an Alabama attorney hired by his father, Loyed pleaded guilty to first-degree murder

Delaware Circuit Court judge Alva Cox asked Loyed if he had "anything to say on [his] own behalf" before a life sentence was imposed.

"No," Key responded.

Later that day, however, Loyed told a *Muncie Star* reporter, "I did not kill my wife, but I pleaded guilty because everyone knows I was there when it happened."

Key said he would have preferred electrocution to the life sentence because "I don't care to live without my wife."

Due to the publicity, Phyllis's case was moved to Grant County.

When Phyllis stood trial that November, Benadum noted that his client had given authorities the information needed to solve the murder mystery.

"But the prosecution didn't give her a nickel's worth of benefit," Benadum said in his opening remarks, revisiting the theme of the Old Testament adultery of David and Bathsheba.

"History is full of love stories," deputy prosecutor Charles "Chic" Clark responded. "They are all passionate affairs. I got my Bible down last weekend and studied it. …And I can quote further, from the Bible, 'Thou shall not kill.'"

On the witness stand, Phyllis again denied she had fired the fatal shots, insisting she had followed her lover's instructions that night and earlier tried to talk Loyed out of killing Ethel.

"But he became like a wild man," she said, "and he threatened to kill me, my ex-husband and himself."

Key—returned from the Indiana State Prison in Michigan City to testify—again implied that Phyllis had killed Ethel, although he indicated he could no longer recall the moments the shots were fired. He also maintained it was Phyllis who rejected his pleas that they should abandon their murder scheme.

Clark introduced notes Hazelbaker had written to Key after their arrests.

"If we can't be together, I'd rather take my own life," she wrote, also suggesting Loyed pursue an insanity defense.

A Wabash gun dealer testified that he recalled selling the murder weapon to Phyllis.

In closing arguments, Benadum again went the Old Testament route and also quoted from *Hamlet*.

"She was infatuated with this man Key," he told jurors. "I don't know what he had, but God knows, men, he must have had something. …Such men as Key have been ruining good women down through the ages. She was under his insane spell."

Grant County prosecutor Robert Foust said he felt "like somebody who won a local talent contest and now has to follow Shakespearean actor Maurice Evans."

That drew a quick response from the seventy-six-year-old Benadum, who had been a player in memorable local trials for a half century.

"I am not a showman or a Shakespearean actor," he insisted. "I'm a plain old one-horse lawyer."

Deputy prosecutor Clark told the jury, "The issue is who was on I-69 and who did the shooting."

"I am convinced it was not David or Bathsheba," he added.

Benadum's co-counsel, Patrick Ryan, said prosecutors "proved again that Loyed Key killed his wife.

"Now they're asking you to send Mrs. Hazelbaker to prison for life because she knew him. He's going to drag her down with him. If someone had thrown incriminating evidence in my car, I'd have thrown it out, too."

The jury deliberated for about six hours. Phyllis quietly wept when it returned a verdict finding her guilty of second-degree murder.

When she was sentenced to life in prison, she said, "I know the jury found me guilty, but I am not guilty of the charge they put upon me."

A newspaper photo showed Hazelbaker consoling her daughter and two sons, all under the age of ten, before she was transported to the Indiana Women's Prison.

Delaware County sheriff Harry Howard and two state police detectives, Donald Hart and George Allen, were later presented with "distinguished service awards" from *True Detective* magazine for their roles in the Key-Hazelbaker investigation.

A *True Detective* article recounting the case was titled, "Six Bullets for Her 13th Anniversary."

In 1967, the Alabama Supreme Court declined to honor a Grant County court order that the four Key children be removed from the custody of their paternal grandparents in the Cotton State and placed in the care of one of Ethel's sisters in Indiana.

Loyed Key died on May 15, 1977, apparently while still incarcerated. Records from the Indiana State Prison do not reflect that he was granted parole before being reclassified as "dead."

Loyed's grave outside Jasper, Alabama—his tombstone declares him "Our beloved father"—is about thirty-five miles from the cemetery where Ethel had been laid to rest a dozen years earlier.

Phyllis Jean Hazelbaker was released on parole sometime after Governor Otis Bowen granted her clemency in 1976.

She was still alive, an eighty-year-old widow leading a quiet life in a small town in southern Indiana, in March 2015, the fiftieth anniversary of the "Happy Anniversary" murder.

14

THE GRAVEL PIT GHOUL

After a World War II veteran and his young bride disappeared in April 1956, leaving behind their toddler children, the good people of Muncie and the surrounding area turned out to help in the search. Even the brother of the missing woman conducted a search by air, piloting a plane in a fruitless attempt to spot their missing car.

No one knew at the time, of course, what a grisly fate had befallen the Spades and how close to home their killer was. Or how true the couple's four-year-old son's statement to police was: "Mommy and Daddy told me they were going to die by a gun."

Early on the morning of April 28, 1956, news broke that forty-two-year-old Darrell Spade and his twenty-four-year-old wife, Mary, had disappeared from their farm in Blackford County, just north of Muncie.

Mary Spade's brother, twenty-two-year-old Chester Schlegel, had been living with the couple and helping with chores on the two-hundred-acre farm. Schlegel had been out late the night before, he said, returning at 2:00 a.m. to discover that his sister and her husband were not home. The children were in their beds, however.

Schlegel said he went to bed for a short time but woke up early to start his duties. He expected to find Darrell Spade in the farm's barn.

When he didn't see his brother-in-law, Schlegel went back to the farmhouse. The Spades were still gone, and their children were in their own beds. Later that morning, Schlegel called police.

The Water Bowl, winter 2016. *Courtesy of Keith Roysdon.*

When police arrived, theories started taking shape. It wasn't unusual for the Spades to put their children to bed and drive to nearby Hartford City. Maybe Darrell Spade, who was known to stop for hitchhikers along the road, had stopped for a drifter. Maybe the hypothetical hitchhiker had kidnapped or otherwise harmed the Spades.

Within hours, an intensive search was on for the Spades and their 1946 brown- and cream-colored Chevrolet. A posse of sixty-five people from the nearby town of Roll—including neighbors and high school students—searched woods in the area.

Chester Schlegel himself piloted a plane over the area in an attempt to spot the Spades' car, and photos of the vehicle were circulated by Indiana State Police.

Sheriff Robert Wentz said he didn't believe the couple had been kidnapped. He noted that while they had a good reputation, they could face child abandonment charges if, as newspapers noted, "they were found alive."

By May 3, however, the case had been turned upside down. Chester Schlegel was arrested for killing Darrell Spade.

But the revelations had only begun.

Indiana dirt road. *Courtesy of Richard Greene, Ball State University archives.*

Investigators show the murder weapons used in the killing of the Spade couple. *Courtesy of Muncie Newspapers Inc.*

The scene as the Spade car was removed from the gravel pit north of Muncie. *Courtesy of Muncie Newspapers Inc.*

Schlegel told police he killed his brother-in-law on the night of April 24—days before they were known to be missing—when he returned home and saw Darrell Spade hitting Mary Spade with a mattock, a pick-like tool.

Schlegel said he then put his sister's dead body and his brother-in-law's freshly made corpse in their car and drove it to a gravel pit near Indiana 3, just north of Muncie. Once there, Schlegel said, he rolled the car into the pit, where it was soon covered with water.

In a grisly scene watched by dozens of onlookers, divers found the car in the gravel pit and pulled it from below the water's surface, rear end first. The bodies of Darrell and Mary Spade were found in the backseat. She was wearing only a nightgown, while he was wearing Levis, army boots and a jacket. The Spades were covered in the backseat by a heavy tarpaulin.

An autopsy indicated that Darrell Spade had been shot below his right ear, while his wife had "a hole in the head…which was presumably dealt with the mattock."

Schlegel's confession, made after he was shown the bodies of his sister and brother-in-law, came after police produced a man who had picked

The bodies of the Spades were in the backseat of their car, covered by a tarp. *Courtesy of Muncie Newspapers Inc.*

up the hitchhiking killer not far from the gravel pit the night he hid their bodies there.

Schlegel tearfully told investigators that he had come home late on the night of April 24 and saw Darrell Spade hitting Mary Spade with the mattock.

Darrell Spade turned and said, "I'll get you next." Schlegel told police he hid in the family's barn, where he found a gun. When Darrell Spade came after him with the mattock, Schlegel said, he shot his brother-in-law.

Schlegel said that his sister was alive despite her head wound, but when he went to the house to get a flashlight and returned, she had died.

Then, rather than calling police, Schlegel decided to dispose of his sister and brother-in-law's bodies himself.

He loaded their remains in their car and drove to the gravel pit just north of Muncie. He put their car into gear and let it roll into the murky waters of the pit, then went to the nearby road and caught a ride home.

Schlegel hid the shotgun in the barn and the mattock in a nearby shed. He poured oil on the bloody ground where his sister's body had lain and dug up the bloody turf where his brother-in-law's body had fallen and "threw it to the hogs."

He said he told the Spades' children, ages four and three, that their parents had left "when the moon was up."

The Spade boy, besides telling police the macabre comment from his parents about how they would "die by a gun," also told investigators, "We will have to wait till Daddy and Mommy come back to life again."

Chester Schlegel and Mary Spade's mother told police that her son and daughter frequently argued about money that Schlegel had loaned to the Spade couple.

Then came a bombshell.

"Coroner Eugene Eissman said Thursday that the examination at Ball Hospital showed water in the woman's lungs, indicating that she was alive when the car bearing their bodies was driven into the quarry, admittedly by Schlegel," the *Muncie Evening Press* reported on May 3, 1956.

Between the time of the murders and his arrest, Schlegel had, improbably, attended services at Dunkirk Church of the Nazarene and told worshippers, "Nobody knows what I'm going through. I know the Lord will take me with Him. I can hardly stand this. There is so much on me. Nobody knows what I'm going through."

Confession and incarceration apparently helped Schlegel's mood, however. In a newspaper article a day later, "Schlegel was reported in good spirits at the Blackford County Jail where he is being held without bond. Friday morning he was reported to have talked and joked with other prisoners and readily taking part in conversation."

As the investigation progressed, new revelations about the relationship between Schlegel and the Spades came to light and new mysteries arose.

Schlegel and family members reinforced the idea that money problems between Darrell and Mary Spade were a frequent point of contention, and investigators increasingly leaned toward the scenario that Schlegel had acted in self-defense when he shot his brother-in-law.

But even while Schlegel reenacted his version of events for investigators, a follow-up visit to the farm several days into May turned up a blood-coated pair of Darrell Spade's eyeglasses. The glasses were found on a sewing table. Schlegel said he had not put them there, but if he did not, who did?

Also found in the farmhouse were books featuring the work of Aristotle, Henry James, Will Durant and Dostoyevsky.

The Spade library "looked like one you might find in the house of a professor of philosophy," one investigator said.

The Spade children were staying at the home of **Charles Spade**, brother of victim Darrell Spade, but Morton Schlegel, **father of Mary Spade** and

Charles Schlegel, indicated that he planned to contest the court-ordered guardianship of Charles Spade.

"God grieves today as we," Reverend Ival Lane said as he delivered the eulogy at Darrell and Mary Spade's funeral services.

When the first criminal charge was filed against Chester Schlegel, it wasn't what the public expected. One week into May 1956, Schlegel was charged with transporting a body across county lines without a permit from the county health officer.

Blackford County authorities took a step that was standard in Indiana in the 1950s: they called a grand jury to consider possible charges against Schlegel.

As Schlegel waited in jail, newspaper accounts noted that he was worried that his fiancée, a young Muncie woman, was thinking of canceling plans for their wedding, which was set for June.

On August 17, 1956, the grand jury returned with several indictments, including second-degree murder, assault and battery. Schlegel was also charged with making a false report to police in connection with his initial call to authorities to claim his sister and brother-in-law had disappeared.

No charge was returned in connection with the death of Mary Spade, but in December 1956, the coroner ruled that her death was caused by suffocation due to drowning. In other words, Mary Spade was alive and breathing, despite her gruesome head wound, when her brother put her in a car and submerged it in the gravel pit.

When he was arrested, Chester Schlegel had a tousled mop of thick black hair, but by the time his trial began in Blackford Circuit Court in February 1957, the now twenty-three-year-old was cleaned up, sporting a "high and tight" haircut that was nearly shaved on the sides of his head. He wore horn-rimmed glasses and a light-colored suit.

As the trial began, authorities read aloud Schlegel's confession, in which he maintained that he shot his brother-in-law in self-defense, as the man, whom Schlegel claimed had just bludgeoned Mary Spade, approached him.

"It was either his life or mine," Schlegel testified during his trial.

Schlegel had always claimed he had fired two shots, but a witness in his trial, a barber who lived less than a mile from the Spade farm, testified he heard three shots that night.

And the Blackford County coroner said his examination of Darrell Spade's body showed that the shots that killed him were fired from behind, contradicting Schlegel's testimony that he shot his brother-in-law as the man approached his hiding place in the barn.

In closing arguments, prosecutor William Ervin told jurors the state believed that Schlegel shot his brother-in-law. When his sister came outside to investigate, Schlegel fired a shot at her—the third shot, heard by the neighbor—and when he missed, he killed her with the mattock. Schlegel then disposed of the bodies in the gravel pit.

Ervin also branded Schlegel with a nickname that stuck.

Schlegel was "a pathological liar and a ghoul of the gravel pit," Ervin said.

The prosecutor also argued that Schlegel might have committed "the perfect crime" if he hadn't been recognized and remembered as he hitchhiked back from the gravel pit.

Schlegel was, shortly after 1:00 a.m. on February 14, 1957, found guilty of second-degree murder in the slaying of his brother-in-law.

"The dark-haired defendant continued chewing gum and showed no emotion when the verdict was read," according to a *Muncie Evening Press* account.

But while Schlegel was awaiting sentencing, authorities reported that he was "losing some of his calm composure, and is showing periods of marked anxiety and depression" in his jail cell.

As the sentencing loomed, Schlegel was visited in jail by his parents.

Three days after the guilty verdict, Judge Victor Simmons sentenced Schlegel to life in prison, adding that he would be eligible for parole in fifteen years.

The twenty-three-year-old maintained he was not guilty.

"I'm as innocent as I can be," Schlegel said. "My only guilt is in transporting the bodies to the gravel pit and lying to the officers at the time. If that is worth fifteen years of my life, so be it. I tried to tell the truth all the time."

Schlegel didn't stop there, however.

"You pulled the wool over the jury's eyes, but you know I am not guilty," he said to prosecutor Ervin and deputy prosecutor Harold Feily.

When you come to the judgment bar of God, I want you to remember that the Bible says the wisest man in the world is the dumbest before God, and that's the way I feel about you two men.

You can take my freedom from me but you can't never take the love of God from my heart and that goes for anyone. I'll forgive anyone who said anything wrong about me and want to thank anyone who tried to help me.

Two days after his sentencing, Schlegel was transported by sheriff's car to the Indiana State Penitentiary in Michigan City.

In July 1956, newspapers reported a late development to the story: more than one thousand people attended an auction of the personal property of Darrell and Mary Spade.

"Some attended the auction Tuesday for reasons of curiosity, but others attended to buy farming implements, grains, livestock, household furnishings and other items of the murdered farm couple," the *Muncie Star* reported. "And the prices bid for such items were reported by sale veterans as very good."

Proceeds from the sale would go into a trust fund the for Spade children, who were living with Darrell Spade's brother.

At the end of the article about the auction, the newspaper reported an intriguing footnote. Authorities in Delaware County, where the gravel pit was located, had considered but decided against pursing charges against Schlegel in relation to the death by drowning of Mary Spade. Since her death had likely occurred in the Delaware County gravel pit, a charge could have been pursued separately from those in Blackford County, the scene of Darrell Spade's death. But no such charge was pursued.

Five years later, the *Muncie Star* reported that the anniversary of the gruesome case had passed with little notice.

"Little has been heard from Schlegel, the two Spade children or other principals in the case in the five years which have followed the double slaying. Only recently, the home of Mr. and Mrs. Morton Schlegel [the defendant's parents] in Jay County burned."

By 1961, the scene of the grisly discovery in the gravel pit had a new purpose. Renamed the Water Bowl, the gravel pit was now a popular swimming and recreation spot north of Muncie. It remained so in 2016.

PUBLIC ENEMY NUMBER ONE

He was America's original celebrity gangster, the first criminal to be referred to—by the media, not the FBI—as "Public Enemy Number One." The capture of Gerald Chapman—in Muncie, of all places—in January 1925 would put the city in front-page headlines nationwide.

It would also eventually cost two Delaware County residents their lives and earn a third a life prison sentence.

Chapman, also known as "the Gentleman Bandit" and "the Count of Gramercy Park," had first won national attention in October 1921, when his gang—including his chief henchman, college-educated George "Dutch" Anderson—pulled off a mail truck robbery in Lower Manhattan.

The holdup, which gave the bandits $2.6 million in cash, bonds and jewels, at the time was the largest robbery in U.S. history.

Chapman became as well known for his dapper, elegant style as he was for his skills as a master of disguise and the nitroglycerin he used to blow open safes.

The feds tracked down Chapman and Anderson in July 1922, and they both were sentenced to twenty-five years in the federal penitentiary in Atlanta for their roles in the postal robbery.

In March 1923, Chapman escaped from the Georgia prison but was quickly recaptured, suffering two gunshot wounds in the process. A few days later, however, he escaped again, this time successfully, from the prison's infirmary.

That December, Anderson would also escape, digging his way under a prison wall.

The murders of Ben and Mary Hance in August 1925 drew national attention because of their apparent connection to notorious gangster Gerald Chapman, who had stayed at the victims' Eaton home. *Courtesy of the* Indianapolis Star.

For more than a year, their whereabouts would be the subject of intense national interest.

Authorities believed the two bandits resurfaced on October 24, 1924, in New Britain, Connecticut, where a city police officer interrupted a store burglary and was fatally shot, reportedly by Chapman.

Investigators in New Britain found some belongings the fleeing bandits left behind, including a travel bag with a tag that identified it as the property of Harry Spickermon, a Muncie physician.

Authorities in Muncie were alerted, and it was eventually determined that Spickermon had treated the bullet wounds Chapman suffered in his failed escape bid. (Local news accounts did not speculate on whether the Muncie doctor knew who his patient was.)

Investigators soon learned Chapman—and Anderson—had spent much of 1924 as tenants living in the farmhouse, just south of Eaton, of Ben and Mary Hance.

Exactly why the gangsters decided to hide out in Delaware County would never officially be determined, but their link to east-central Indiana would appear to be Charles "One-Arm" Wolf, a former Hartford City police officer who turned to a life of crime after a tragedy in his home in March 1921.

Law enforcement colleagues in Blackford County said they had to repeatedly stop Wolf from trying to take his own life after his revolver accidentally discharged, sending a .38-caliber bullet into the face of his wife, Frances, killing her instantly. (Wolf had lost his right hand and forearm a few years earlier in yet another accidental shooting.)

The grief-stricken Wolf resigned from the police force in the wake of his wife's death. Over the next three years, he would become the target of criminal investigations, facing charges ranging from liquor law violations to auto theft.

In a 1922 case filed in Delaware County, Ben Hance—two years before he provided lodging for Chapman and Anderson—was accused of hiding car tires, which had been stolen by Wolf, on his Eaton farm.

How Wolf came into contact with Chapman is unclear. (Perhaps not coincidentally, a woman who lived with Chapman in New York City prior to the postal robbery was from Indiana.) Some have speculated that it was Wolf who was waiting near the federal penitentiary when Chapman escaped and drove the "Gentleman Bandit" from Georgia to the Hoosier State.

At some point in their probe of Chapman's activities in the Muncie area, local authorities began to receive the assistance of Hance, the gangster's landlord.

They learned that during his stay on the Eaton farm, Chapman enjoyed taking target practice at a large tree outside the farmhouse and fishing in the nearby Mississinewa River.

(The officers also came to believe Chapman had used nitro to blow open safes at Eaton's two banks and Stillman's Department Store in downtown Muncie.)

It was determined Chapman had spent a considerable amount of time in Muncie beyond his visits to Dr. Spickermon's office, dining at downtown restaurants, playing cards at a cigar store and at times staying at the Braun Hotel. And it would be on the streets of downtown Muncie that Chapman would take his final steps as a free man.

He was walking along East Charles Street, near the current site of the YWCA, on the morning of Sunday, January 18, 1925, when four men approached him on the pretense of asking for directions. By the time he realized they were police officers, it was too late.

Chapman tried to get off a shot, but his gun apparently misfired. "Damn the man who turned me up for blood money," he said as his captors led him away.

(For the record, along with his pistol, Chapman had two bottles of nitroglycerin and $4,963 in cash when apprehended.)

The bandit, almost immediately driven to Indianapolis for security reasons, soon found himself back in Connecticut, to stand trial—and face a possible death sentence—in the police officer's slaying.

When he stood trial that April, it set the stage for a reunion with Ben Hance, whose testimony about a vehicle driven by his former house guest apparently helped link Chapman to the New Britain killing.

The Eaton farmer also maintained that he knew Chapman as "Tom Miller."

"I know this probably means my life," Hance told guards assigned to protect him in New Jersey. "But I have to clear my conscience."

The jury found Chapman guilty, and he was sentenced to death—although his execution would be delayed for a year as his attorneys exhausted the appeals process.

While Chapman awaited his fate, life perhaps returned to something approaching normal for a presumably relieved Ben Hance and his spouse.

Different reasons were offered for what prompted the Hances to be traveling west on the Middletown Pike—generally following the same route Indiana 67 now cuts through southwestern Delaware County—on the afternoon of Friday, August 14, 1925.

Some said they were delivering peas—or perhaps eggs—to a customer who had placed an order over the telephone Chapman had installed in their Eaton farmhouse.

The couple had made it as far as Salem Township when a car began tailing their vehicle in the area of Delaware County Road 600-W.

That vehicle—authorities would later say it was driven by "One-Arm" Wolf—would pass the Hance car and then cut it off.

The Hances, who realized what was unfolding, tried to flee on foot.

A gunman—almost certainly "Dutch" Anderson—killed the barefoot Mary Hance instantly with a shot through her head. She fell at the side of the road.

Her husband, meanwhile, ran into a nearby cornfield after two of Anderson's bullets tore through his abdomen.

A few minutes later, the mortally wounded Hance emerged from the field and approached farmer Charles Cromer. He collapsed, got to his feet and then went down a second time.

"They got me," he reportedly told the horrified Cromer. "Charles Wolf and Dutch Anderson."

Asked why he had been shot, Hance said, "On account of Gerald Chapman."

Ben Hance lived for about forty-five minutes after being shot. He apparently made several comments to police and emergency personnel, most of them from nearby Middletown, who had raced to the scene.

Charles "One-Arm" Wolf, fourth from left, stands with local police following his August 1925 arrest in the slayings of an Eaton couple. *Courtesy of Muncie Newspapers Inc.*

Nearly all would say he identified Anderson as his killer. A few would later maintain that they never heard the dying man mention Wolf's name.

Hance, rushed to Muncie's Home Hospital, repeatedly asked to speak to Fred Puckett, one of the Muncie Police Department detectives who had collared Chapman.

By the time Puckett reached the south-side hospital, however, Hance had lost consciousness. He would say no more.

Wolf—who at the time apparently lived along Wysor Street in Muncie—was arrested by city police a few hours later. He maintained he knew nothing about that afternoon's mayhem.

A massive search for "Dutch" Anderson turned up nothing. (Reports later in the summer that he had been tracked to a cottage on Lake Webster in northern Indiana proved false.)

Like the capture of Chapman seven months earlier, the Hance slayings were reported in front-page stories from coast to coast. Many of the stories blamed the killings on a man incarcerated about eight hundred miles from the crime scene.

"Through prison bars and across one-fourth a continent, Gerald Chapman has wreaked vengeance on those who betrayed him," read one widely circulated United Press International account.

A few days later, from his death row cell in Connecticut, Chapman issued a statement through his attorney.

"I've known Anderson for a long time, and he's incapable of such a rotten deal, particularly after the kind treatment Mrs. Hance accorded Anderson and myself when we stayed with them," he said.

> *Many times when either of us was sick, she took care of us, showing the kindness of a mother.*
>
> *I can't conceive Anderson shooting a woman in cold blood. Anderson and I left Muncie with the best of feeling towards the farmer and his wife. I have never had occasion to change my feeling towards them. Hance testified against me here, but he had to.*

Chapman also said he couldn't imagine why Anderson "would be within 1,000 miles of that place."

("The bandit prince'" presumably would have been equally dismissive of reports that Anderson burned down a large auto repair shop in Steubenville, Ohio, after an employee's testimony at the New Britain trial helped document Chapman's travels in the wake of the officer's slaying.)

With Anderson nowhere to be found, Delaware County prosecutor Van Ogle made plans to bring his co-defendant, Wolf, to trial alone.

Before the trial began, however, Anderson's participation became a moot point. On the night of October 31—Halloween—Anderson exchanged gunshots with a police detective in Muskegon, Michigan, after trying to pass a counterfeit twenty-dollar bill at a local store.

Both men died of their bullet wounds.

When testimony began a few days later at Wolf's trial in Muncie, Prosecutor Ogle's star witnesses were those who recounted hearing the dying Ben Hance identify his assailants by name.

"Ben Hance told the truth as he lay mortally wounded along that country road last August," the prosecutor said, "if he ever told the truth."

Also testifying for the state were a group of Yorktown citizens who maintained they had seen Wolf and a second man driving through that community—four miles from the slaying scene—only a few minutes after the Hances were gunned down.

Wolf, for his part, insisted he had never left Muncie on the afternoon of August 14.

Defense attorney John O'Neill called to the stand a series of witnesses who said they clearly recalled seeing Wolf—at specific times, virtually to the minute—that afternoon, all at locations a considerable distance from the Middletown Pike.

One of those defense witnesses was former Muncie mayor Rollin Bunch, who recalled Wolf had been at his East Jackson Street medical office that afternoon to pick up medication.

Some pundits later suggested O'Neill called too many alibi witnesses.

In his closing remarks, Ogle said those testifying for the defense were tied to Wolf by "personal friendships." He also suggested the defendant would have "had to have been a bird, or to have had an airplane," to have been at all of the locations described by those witnesses.

(The attorneys nearly came to blows at one point in the trial, after Ogle asked a witness to confirm that O'Neill had purchased a car from Gerald Chapman. The incensed defense attorney called the prosecutor a "cur.")

In the end, the jury deliberated for less than three hours before finding Wolf guilty of murder.

Ogle had urged them to issue a death sentence, but they decided instead on a sentence of life imprisonment—likely because of the general belief that Anderson, not Wolf, had fired the fatal shots.

When the jury's verdict was returned, Wolf turned to his ten-year-old son, Guy, and said, "I am not guilty."

He later made the same remark when Judge Clarence Dearth formally imposed the life sentence.

In Connecticut, Gerald Chapman's death sentence was upheld by appellate courts.

"The Gentleman Bandit" was executed—through the use of a neck-breaking device known as the "upright jerker"—at 12:04 a.m. on April 6, 1926.

In the wake of Chapman's execution, a song about his troubled life, "Gerald Chapman, What a Pity," enjoyed brief popularity.

No songs were written about "One-Arm" Wolf, now a resident of the Indiana State Prison in Michigan City.

Not long after Wolf's arrival at the prison, another inmate from Muncie, Eddie Duffy, made headlines by claiming a local man who had testified against him in a robbery trial was the true killer of the Hances.

Prosecutor Ogle investigated and said he determined Duffy's claim was "ridiculous."

"A dying man, who knows he is dying, does not accuse anybody falsely," Ogle said.

The Wolf case would briefly return to the news in 1927, when there was an impeachment trial for Judge Dearth in the Indiana Senate. One of the allegations against the Muncie jurist—who survived the attempt to oust him from the bench—was that rules had been violated when prospective jurors for the Wolf trial were selected.

For years after his conviction, "One-Arm" Wolf's family continued to pursue vindication for him—or at the very least, a chance at eventual freedom.

His minister brother, Perry Wolf, called Charles "a kind-hearted and industrious man and a great friend of the Hances."

"I am positive he never consorted with 'Dutch' Anderson or Gerald Chapman," the pastor added.

In March 1941, Indiana governor Henry Schricker, in part citing the defendant's good behavior while incarcerated, commuted Wolf's sentence from life to eighteen years.

Wolf was released in 1943 and moved to Dundee, Florida, where he lived with his sister and brother-in-law and worked for a time as a fruit buyer.

"Charlie never talked to me about his life up north," his sister would later tell a newspaper reporter. When he would drink, though, Wolf would sometimes boast that he had $120,000 in cash hidden back in Indiana.

"One-Arm's" son, Guy, who had also relocated to Florida, was only thirty-six when he died in 1951.

In March 1957, *Reader's Digest* published a condensed version of a book about Chapman's criminal exploits: *The Count of Gramercy Park*.

Wolf, depicted in the story, wasn't happy about the late-in-life exposure.

A Florida newspaper later recounted that he had "haunted" newsstands in the Dundee area, buying as many copies of that month's *Digest* as he could find, trying to keep his past out of the view of his friends and neighbors.

By June 1959, it appeared that Wolf, now sixty-seven, was again making questionable choices about those with whom he kept company.

The first week of that month, the senior citizen spent four days in a Bartow, Florida hospital, recovering from injuries that had apparently been suffered in a severe beating.

That June 23, a low-income neighborhood in Dundee—not especially close to Wolf's home—was rocked by an explosion that destroyed a vacant cottage there.

"One-Arm" Wolf was found in the front yard, suffering from severe burns that would quickly end his life. Inside, authorities found the charred remains of a twenty-seven-year-old local man.

A cause for the blast—and an explanation for what the men were doing there—was apparently never provided.

MUST SPEND LIFE IN STATE PRISON

Charles (One-Arm) Wolf

TERROR GRIPS

Charles "One-Arm" Wolf received a life sentence for the Hance slayings but was paroled in the early 1940s. He died in a mysterious explosion in Florida in 1959. *Courtesy of the Muncie Newspapers Inc.*

The Gerald Chapman saga remained in the public consciousness for decades after his capture and execution.

When two of the Muncie police officers who had captured Chapman in 1925 died—Fred Puckett in 1943 and Merv Collins in 1952—national wire stories that noted their connection to the case appeared in publications across the country.

By the later decades of the twentieth century, however, with the key players in the drama long gone, Chapman and his story largely faded from the nation's collective memory—even in Muncie and Delaware County. Nine decades later, stories about the Public Enemy Number One who hid out in an Eaton farmhouse and fished the Mississinewa are still occasionally told by old-timers.

But in most of those tellings, the protagonist is no longer Gerald Chapman. Instead, Chapman's local exploits are erroneously credited to an entirely different gangster, who did pass through Muncie and east-central Indiana nearly a decade after the "Count of Gramercy Park's" ill-fated stroll down East Charles Street. A fellow from Mooresville, by the name of Dillinger.

The Ghosts of Muncie

A city with a history as violent as Muncie's has more than a few ghosts. Most of them, however, are the ghosts of dashed hopes, wayward lives and justice gone awry. There are some real ghost stories, however, lingering in Muncie's dark places and in the city's historic spots. And there's no spot in Muncie more conducive to communing with those who have passed on than Beech Grove Cemetery.

The final resting place to more than forty-two thousand people, Beech Grove is a city-owned cemetery covering one hundred acres along White River. Chartered in 1841, when Muncie itself was barely a town, Beech Grove includes the graves of Revolutionary War, Civil War and War of 1812 veterans.

As was common practice for decades, the cemetery was segregated. The Beech Grove website notes that there were separate sections for Jews and Catholics—unmentioned is that there was a section for local African Americans buried there—and the poor.

The section of pauper graves at Beech Grove, where the poor and indigent are still buried at county expense, is at the bottom of a hill from the graves and tombs of some of the city's richest families, then–cemetery superintendent Tom Schnuck noted in early 2016.

But Schnuck said Beech Grove has no ghosts or ghost stories to tell.

Tell that to the young adventure-seekers who comment online about exploring the cemetery and seeking out spirits. Websites contain pictures of interesting and eerie monuments experienced throughout Beech Grove.

Rivoli Theater. *Courtesy of the Ball State University archives.*

There's little doubt that the Beech Grove trustees who wrote the cemetery's 1906 handbook would approve. The handbook, which tells the history of the cemetery's first half century, sets down firm rules governing Beech Grove.

The rules include prohibitions of smoking, obscene language or intoxicated people on the cemetery grounds. And the very first rule is one that wouldn't seem necessary, but the trustees apparently felt it was: "No person shall inter any dead body in the cemetery, except under the supervision of the superintendent or assistant superintendent."

Even though Beech Grove has a notable lack of ghost stories, other places in Muncie have persistent legends of hauntings.

On the campus of Ball State University, Elliott Hall is one of the most easily identifiable "haunted" spots in the city and has been for decades. It is named for Frank Elliott Ball, one of the children of Frank C. Ball, whose family established the university. Frank Elliott Ball died in a plane crash in 1936.

Elliott Hall was built and opened to male students in 1938, but their ranks were depleted when young men fought in World War II.

When returning soldiers turned scholars came to Ball State after the war, the tragedy that gave Elliott Hall its haunted reputation occurred, according to an Elliott Hall page on the university's website:

Elliott Hall. *Courtesy of the Ball State University archives.*

On January 26, 1947, resident and WWII veteran William Carl Schaumberg hanged himself from the rafters in the fourth floor library. Schaumberg was part of a US Army reintroduction program. He had been horribly disfigured in the war and felt shunned from his fellow students, his family and his fiancée. Upon returning from winter break, he took his own life.

Residents of Elliott Hall have embraced the legend. The website notes that the Elliott Hall "haunted house tradition" began in 1975.

Muncie Civic Theater, a performing arts theater in downtown Muncie, is more than a century old and has been restored in recent years. But there were times during its history when the then-dilapidated building was home to more ghosts than performers and playgoers.

Muncie Civic Theater. *Courtesy of the Ball State University archives.*

The *Ball State Daily News* reported in October 2015 that ghost-hunting investigators toured the theater and were startled at one point when their equipment detected an invisible figure walking toward them in the basement.

The newspaper quoted then–general manager Chris Griffith as he recounted a story about a man who killed himself in an upstairs room after his daughter died.

Griffith added a macabre note: "At night one time, I could hear a skipping, like a little girl would, on the floor where he would have lived at the time."

If any building still intact downtown rivals the theater building for haunted history, it is the former Roberts Hotel, which opened in 1921 but closed as a place for lodging in 2006 and was gutted, remodeled and reopened in 2014 as apartments.

For several years after the hotel closed, workmen and a few curious people who had the necessary connections to the key holder were the only ones to get inside the Roberts.

A few people stayed overnight in the dark, cavernous hotel during those years and reported hearing—something. Noises. Movement where there shouldn't be any.

An undated postcard for the Roberts Hotel. *Courtesy of the Ball State University archives.*

Maybe they were hearing the hotel's ghost, whose story was told in a booklet published when the hotel was first revived in 1987. Frederick Graham wrote a multi-page history of the hotel that touched on not only the hotel's former glamour but also its darker history.

The Roberts had hosted dignitaries and celebrities like movie star Joan Crawford, national political figure Wendell Wilkie, Bob Hope, presidential candidate John F. Kennedy and First Lady Eleanor Roosevelt. All stayed overnight, the booklet said.

"Another 'guest' at the hotel is not so much colorful as mysterious," according to the Roberts booklet.

> *This "guest" is seen occasionally on dark, moonless nights when the streets near the hotel are unusually quiet.*
>
> *Passersby will see what appears to be a woman peering out one of the windows. Something about this sight especially attracts and holds the eye of the beholder. Some have described it as a young woman, dressed in neat, dark schoolmarm-type clothes.*
>
> *She will be quite motionless and her appearance always arouses curiosity. Invariably the thing is at the window of a room not believed to be occupied. After each such sighting an inspection will be made of the room where the vision appeared but no one has ever been found.*

Upon repeated sightings with no explanation of the phenomena and no ill effects, it has been decided that she is a very refined ghost, the likes of which every hotel should possess.

Could this apparition be the spirit of the Muncie librarian who plunged to her death from her room? The young woman often stayed a few days at the hotel. This grim happening was during World War II, on the night of Jan. 4, 1943, when Muncie lay in complete darkness for the town's first blackout test.

On that night, the librarian was in a sixth-floor room. It is believed that she put on her winter coat against the cold night, opened the window of her room, leaned far out to check on the results of the blackout, slipped and fell to her death. The accident was discovered by a warden who was checking on compliance of the blackout.

One of the most intriguing—but quickly disproved—of Muncie's ghost stories is the story of Milo Snell. Snell, who died in 1980 at the age of seventy-five, was a film projectionist for most of his life.

According to his obituary on August 29, 1980, Snell worked as a projectionist at the Wysor and Rivoli Theaters in downtown Muncie for forty-nine years.

"As a child, he assisted his father by manually operating film projectors before the days of electrically operated equipment," his obituary noted.

The Rivoli, which opened in 1927, was one of several movie theaters in downtown Muncie during the heyday of urban movie houses. Its main floor and balcony were often filled with kids and adults enjoying the latest "picture show." *Gone with the Wind* played at the Rivoli after its 1939 release and returned when the movie was reissued to theaters a final time in the 1970s.

The Rivoli was demolished in 1987 to make way for an office building, but before the wrecking ball swung, local photographer and historian John Disher went through the Rivoli one last time, documenting as much as he could before the end.

That included addressing the legend of Milo Snell's ghost.

On his website, Disher recounts his opportunity to tour the Rivoli during its final days, talk to the employees and the manager and hear stories about Snell, who kept a basement workshop. Snell was a projectionist but also a theater handyman who could fix almost anything, Disher was told.

And Disher heard stories that Milo's ghost still roamed the hidden recesses of the Rivoli, seven years after he died.

A chair in a hidden room at the Rivoli Theater. *Courtesy of John Disher.*

"Indeed, during my visit, lights in the basement workshop area would inexplicably turn themselves off and on," Disher wrote.

Disher entered a small room in the basement that was part of the air-handling system. Inside this metal room were a couple of chairs, including one that Rivoli employees said was Milo Snell's projection room chair.

Disher bought the chair a few days later, during an auction of the theater's contents. It has been in his house since 1987.

He noted, jokingly, that the chair has never manifested any supernatural properties in all those years. But Disher expressed disappointment in 2015, when he was told by former manager Dave Battas that the chair "probably" didn't belong to Milo Snell.

It made for a good story, though, as did the story of Milo's ghost.

THE CURIOUS CASE OF DR. ROSS

When Muncie physician Nelson B. Ross was arrested for fatally shooting a streetcar conductor in October 1909, after a dispute over ten cents, it likely didn't do much to diminish his reputation.

For the better part of a decade, Ross had been the subject of headlines, many of them scandalous. As the *Muncie Evening Press* reported, his slaying of conductor Daniel Linder only "marked the climax of a long string of sensational episodes."

Since hanging out his shingle in 1897, Ross had twice been the target of federal criminal investigations involving mail. In one, he was accused of stealing ninety-two dollars from a letter that had been intended for another Nelson Ross. In the other, he was charged with sending material to a St. Louis woman that authorities deemed to be pornography.

He was accused of shoving his ex-wife down a flight of stairs.

At least twice, he faced criminal charges after allegedly performing what were referred to as "illegal operations"—abortions—in which his patients died.

When one of those cases put his medical license at risk in 1906, Ross told a reporter that anyone trying to shut down his practice would "get all he is looking for and possibly more."

Ross also "intimated that a shotgun and a 60-pound bulldog might be used to good advantage."

In August 1907, Ross's much younger girlfriend died suddenly, minutes after he had left her family's Farmland home. Her parents, who hadn't

Nelson Ross, a Muncie physician and convicted killer, near the end of his turbulent life. *Courtesy of the Muncie Newspapers Inc.*

approved of the relationship, made "grave" accusations that he was somehow responsible.

A year later, when a "medicine vendor" set up shop at Charles and Walnut Streets and proclaimed the benefits of his remedies to a rapidly growing crowd that gathered, the physician—who lived and worked in the nearby Jones Building—emerged with a megaphone.

After being shouted down by Ross, the medicine man alerted police and accused the doctor of interference with a public meeting. Ross, meanwhile, accused the vendor of blockading a sidewalk. Both men were arrested.

In early 1909, Ross's correspondence had him in hot water again. When a local streetcar motorman, O.A. Ellman, showed up at the doctor's office to express his unhappiness with a letter his wife had received from Ross, the physician struck him several times.

Ross, who maintained that the irate husband had insulted a young woman in his office, was found guilty of assault and battery.

The troubled physician came from a respected local family. Ross's father was also a medical doctor and a leading advocate for prohibition. His brother, Ralph, was a Muncie attorney.

Many suspected his connections were responsible for Nelson Ross always seeming to avoid much in the way of consequences after trouble came his way.

Ross finally went too far on Thursday, October 5, 1909.

That morning, Ross made a house call at the home of a patient in Desoto, about seven miles northeast of downtown Muncie. For reasons never explained, before he boarded the streetcar that morning, Ross failed to buy a ticket.

Once on board and with the the trip under way, Ross was informed of a Muncie & Portland Traction Co. policy that, as a passenger with no ticket, he would be required to pay the full fare for a trip to Portland: twenty cents.

A ticket to Desoto would have cost the doctor a dime.

Ross was outraged over the ten-cent penalty, exchanging angry words with the streetcar's crew. While at his patient's house, a witness would later recall, the doctor predicted there would be a "hell of a fight" on his ride home that afternoon and said someone could get shot.

On the trip home, Ross again quarreled with crew members over his morning fare. After the physician threatened to punch one of the workers, conductor Linder pulled a "bell rope," stopping the car, and told Ross he would be given back the ten cents he had paid for his trip to Muncie and asked him to get off.

After Ross declined to leave, four crew members removed him from the car, which had stopped near Holt's Crossing, not far from the present site of the Muncie Bypass.

By all accounts but one—that of Ross—he was the only man off the car, with the employees standing on a rear platform, when he produced a handgun, held with both hands.

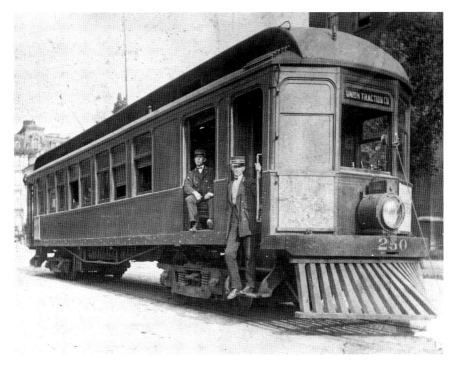

After a decade of controversies and scandals, Nelson Ross fatally shot a local streetcar conductor in a dispute over a ten-cent fare. *Courtesy of Ball State University archives.*

Witnesses would later testify that before he began shooting, Ross snarled, "Put me off, will you?"

The first bullet hit no one. The second struck the twenty-nine-year-old Linder just below his left armpit. The projectile tore through his left lung and pierced his heart. A third bullet was then fired, passing through his left leg.

The mortally wounded conductor stepped off the other side of the platform and began to run for the front of the car. He didn't make it far before collapsing. "Boys, I guess I'm shot" were his last words. Female passengers screamed.

Ross reentered the car, seemingly intent on shooting the other crew members. Women on board pleaded with him to leave.

Witnesses said Ross walked away, going into a wooded area, after being told Linder was dead—but only after urging those on the streetcar to testify that the conductor had been wearing brass knuckles.

Ross was arrested later that afternoon by two city police officers riding bicycles, after they saw him in a taxicab at Monroe and Jackson Streets.

At the time of his arrest in 1909, Nelson Ross had his medical office, and an apartment, in what was then known as the Jones Building at Walnut and Charles Streets. *Courtesy of Ball State University archives.*

A grand jury would soon indict him on charges of murder and attempted murder.

Newspaper accounts described the physician loudly playing a harmonica in his cell at the Delaware County jail, performing standards that included "Home Sweet Home" and "I Wish I Had a Girl," a big hit for entertainer Billy Murray the previous May.

The day of Linder's funeral, all streetcars in the Muncie area stopped for three minutes at 10:00 a.m. The traction company provided Delaware County prosecutor Harry Long with two attorneys to assist in the case.

The Ross trial drew standing-room-only crowds. The defendant's parents, who were divorced, sat at the defense table, along with his two sisters.

Seated with prosecutors were Linder's wife, their two young sons and the victim's parents. The young widow collapsed and fainted when her husband's shooting was recounted in opening arguments.

Testimony about the conductor's killing was fairly consistent until the thirty-seven-year-old Ross took the stand. He tearfully maintained he was being roughed up by the crew when he fired in self-defense. "Someone then hit me with something hard, and I then reached to my belt and pulled my gun," he said.

Deputy prosecutor William A. Thompson asked Ross whether he had indeed been arrested twelve previous times on a variety of charges. The physician didn't respond.

Police and coroner Aaron Cecil testified that they found no brass knuckles in Linder's possession—although after the autopsy, a pair was found in a previously inspected coat belonging to the conductor.

Two reporters and a lawyer who had been at the morgue that day were called to the stand and asked what they knew about the sudden appearance of the brass knuckles.

Prosecutors called sixteen witnesses to the stand who said they were aware of Ross's bad reputation. They included physicians, several business owners and police officers, as well as *Evening Press* editor Wilbur Sutton.

Long said jurors should sentence Ross to death by hanging, saying it would rid the county of a "great burden." Defense attorney Walter Ball urged the jury—composed of eleven farmers, seven of them from Henry County, and an "oil agent"—to find his client guilty of manslaughter.

"Dr. Ross bore no malice against any of the traction employees, and the shooting occurred during the intense heat of his anger," Ball said.

At first, four jurors voted for execution, but the panel eventually found Ross guilty of second-degree murder, imposing a life sentence.

At his formal sentencing hearing, Ross was asked if he had anything to say.

"Nothing, other than I don't think the evidence in the case warranted the verdict that was returned," he responded.

Nelson Ross's transfer to the Indiana State Prison in Michigan City did not mark the end of his story. For decades after his incarceration, the now-former physician and his relatives applied to Hoosier governors for a pardon. Such efforts met with strong resistance from the survivors of Daniel Linder.

In November 1914, Ross's mother called on Governor Samuel Ralston, tearfully urging him to "send my boy home" and presenting him with a poem Ross had composed in his prison cell. Its title was "A Lifer's Plea."

"I toil all day and dream all night," Ross wrote in the first of five stanzas. "For I am in prison, the result of a fight. I am getting old, and my hair is turning gray. My life is slowly ebbing away." The rhyming phrases did not move Ralston to the degree that he issued a pardon.

In January 1926, Ross was released from the state prison—but for only thirty days so he could visit his ailing mother.

When his thirty-day parole expired, Ross was nowhere to be found. He was captured several weeks later in St. Louis, where he was living under an assumed name, working as a wealthy man's private nurse.

Ross's final bid for clemency was rejected in October 1937 by a prison board that noted he had been cited for numerous conduct violations.

The following May, however, Governor M. Clifford Thompson issued what at first was a temporary pardon, after being told that Ross's health was declining rapidly.

The convicted killer lived in Indianapolis with his sister, Lena, who later reported he had enjoyed attending horse races at the state fair and movies.

His health continued to fail, however, and in December 1938, he voluntarily returned to the state prison, telling family members that the physicians in in the infirmary there were familiar with his case and would provide him with "the best of treatment." He died there, at the age of sixty-six, on February 7, 1939.

His sister told the *Indianapolis News* that Ross's fondest wish, "to return to Muncie for four or five years, renew acquaintances and die a free man," had not been granted.

In his *Muncie Evening Press* column, editor Sutton—who had testified about Ross's bad reputation at the 1909 murder trial—wrote that "Doc Ross was not all bad. Probably nobody is. …His principal fault was a temper that he could apparently not restrain."

After his death at the Indiana State Prison in 1939, Nelson Ross was returned to his hometown for burial in Beech Grove Cemetery. *Courtesy of Douglas Walker.*

Ross's family buried him, next to his mother, in Beech Grove Cemetery and posthumously returned a designation he had formally been stripped of three decades earlier. On his tombstone, he is identified for posterity as "Nelson B. Ross, M.D."

Brutal Death in a Tavern

In the middle of the twentieth century, a Muncie tavern was not a safe place to be.

It's little wonder that not until 1969 was Indiana law changed to allow women to actually sit at the bar in a tavern instead of at a table. The previous ban, quaint and outdated now, was supposed to protect "the fairer sex" from the worst taverns had to offer.

But no amount of protection—not even an off-duty police officer on hand at the time of the attack—was enough to save Mildred Sexton the night she was all but decapitated in a Muncie bar.

Even before Sexton's gruesome death, taverns in Muncie were known for the violence often unleashed when their working-class patrons got bellies full of whiskey and heads full of anger.

In March 1965, deputy prosecutor A.J. Hall told a jury in a murder trial, "Until a few years ago, Delaware County had a reputation of being a place where you could kill a man and get away with it."

Hall was urging jurors to impose a lengthy prison sentence on James Mullenix, a twenty-eight-year-old Muncie man who had, a year earlier, slit the throat of Willie Oscar Price Jr. moments after Price walked into the Magic City Tavern on South Walnut Street.

Mullenix's defense attorney portrayed Price and his two companions as "three men who were fatally bent on mischief that morning."

The defense hinged on the argument that Price himself brought the knife to the Magic City Tavern, but it was turned on him.

Mullenix was ultimately found guilty of manslaughter and handed a prison sentence ranging from two to twenty-one years.

Muncie police reassured citizens that they would clean up the city's taverns.

In 1969, Muncie police captain Paul Singer—referred to in newspaper accounts as "the thorn in the side of certain Muncie tavern operators"—was the overnight shift supervisor for the department. As such, Singer commanded the patrolmen who responded to calls about robberies, thefts, stabbings and other incidents in local taverns—especially the rough hangouts along Walnut Street downtown and just south of downtown.

Delaware County deputy prosecutor A.J. Hall. *Courtesy of Ball State University archives.*

In March 1969, Singer paid what he called a "last friendly visit" to the city's taverns. Singer and his officers were looking for bartenders without liquor licenses, making sure that each establishment had a copy of the state Alcoholic Beverage Commission rules and that bar owners knew when to close up for the night. By 2:30 a.m., taverns had to be closed. The only people who could be in the bars after that time were the closer and cleaning man.

Coincidentally—or not—the Muncie police action came just as state law changed how women could be patrons of bars throughout the state.

In its 1969 session, the Indiana legislature changed the law to allow women to sit at the bar in a tavern. Previously, women could sit only in a booth in a tavern.

When the law was passed, the *Muncie Star* newspaper sent a female reporter to local bars to see how bartenders and patrons would react.

The reporter, Dee McKinsey, wrote that her editor "patted me on the head" and sent her out to pull up a stool to local bars. "Walking into a tavern alone is one thing, but actually charging up to the bar is something else entirely," she wrote.

What reaction did she get?

"You know, you are the first lady we have had at this bar," one bartender told her. Another bartender laughed and walked into the back room; the tavern owner came back out and told her they would never serve a woman at the bar. In another bar, she was welcomed, and in another, she was served "in stoic silence."

"In all four cocktail lounges, the patrons were obviously aghast, but once the novelty wore off, they were returned to their drinks and conversation which my entrance had interrupted," she wrote.

In many quarters, Muncie had little mercy for women at this time. A couple months after the reporter made her foray into local bars, three accused wife murderers appeared in Delaware Circuit Court on a single day. Two were sentenced, and one was changing his plea to guilty.

One of those being sentenced was Marvin Hollis Sexton, who, more than four years earlier, had killed his wife, Mildred Hazel Sexton, in an attack in a tavern that was so brutal, people in Muncie were still talking about it for decades.

On a hot night in July 1965, twenty-seven-year-old Marvin Sexton strode angrily into the Yorkshire Tavern in the 1100 block of South Walnut Street. His wife, twenty-three-year-old Mildred, was sitting in a booth with a man.

The Sextons were first cousins, and since they were married in 1959, they'd had six children.

But the two, who had moved to Muncie from Tennessee, had separated. Mildred had filed for divorce six months earlier.

After Marvin Sexton got into an argument with his wife, off-duty Muncie police officer James Peters, who was working at the bar, told him to leave.

He did but returned at about midnight with a knife with a four-inch blade.

Sexton crossed the bar floor in a few steps and approached his wife from behind, grabbing her by the hair, pulling her head back and cutting her throat several times. The slashes severed a major vein and a major artery, as well as her trachea. In a subsequent court hearing, authorities said her head was about an inch and a half from total decapitation.

Peters quickly ran around the bar and grabbed Marvin Sexton, subduing him by hitting the killer with a lead-filled "sap" and then, when he couldn't wrestle the knife out of Marvin Sexton's hand, driving the blade into the killer's own leg.

Although authorities cite varying numbers of onlookers, it's possible one hundred people were in the bar that night.

Ripples from the brutal slaying began spreading immediately. Mildred's brother, Seigal Bobby Sexton—he had the same last name as his sister even after she married because the Sexton husband and wife were cousins—had been shot in the hip by a Muncie police officer just a few days earlier. Despite his injury, he escaped from police. But after his sister was killed, Seigal Sexton turned himself in to police so he could attend Mildred's funeral.

As was standard in Muncie at the time, prosecutors let members of a grand jury decide if Marvin Sexton should be indicted for his wife's murder. Defense attorney Dick Clapp represented the wife killer.

The grand jury returned an indictment of first-degree murder after hearing testimony from witnesses, including Officer Peters.

(At some point between Mildred's slaying and the grand jury indictment, Muncie newspapers began referring to what they had been calling the Yorkshire Lounge as Rocky's Showboat, the name by which the bar was best known for years. It was not the last name change for the tavern, as we'll see.)

Within a month of the slaying, however, twists and turns in the case meant changes in how the prosecution of Marvin Sexton would play out.

Defense attorney Clapp hired two Muncie physicians to examine the killer and determine if he was "suffering a temporary unsoundness of mind when his wife was killed and is, therefore, not guilty of first-degree murder."

Prosecutor Frederick McClellan quickly filed a denial of Clapp's insanity defense argument, and circuit court judge Alva Cox hired a third doctor to examine Sexton, who was being held without bail in the Delaware County Jail.

In October, less than three months after his wife's killing, Marvin Sexton was committed to Norman Beatty State Hospital in Westville, Indiana. Reports from the physicians who examined him had been split on whether he was insane.

"Would the person charged kill in the presence of a police officer?" Clapp had argued. "I submit that he did just that in the presence of a uniformed policeman and fifteen other witnesses."

Judge Cox agreed, ruling that Sexton "lacks sufficient comprehension" of the crime and the charge against him and ordered that Sexton be committed.

Four years later, in early 1969, doctors at the Westville hospital sent Judge Cox a report saying that Sexton was now mentally able to stand trial.

By this point, William Bruns was the deputy prosecutor on the case, and Donald Chiappetta had replaced Clapp as Sexton's public defender.

Sexton underwent sixty-five electro-shock treatments while at the hospital, which impaired his memory of the night of the slaying, Chiappetta said.

Testimony during Sexton's 1969 trial indicated that he not only confessed to killing his wife but also appeared to be "calm and cool."

"I just did the big one," Sexton was quoted as saying. "I killed the old bitch. It's funny what a man can do in five seconds. I've done it. I'm glad she's dead. I'll sleep tonight and tomorrow and tomorrow night."

Sexton then gave an officer four dimes to buy a pack of cigarettes for him. He told the cops that by the time he finished the pack of cigarettes, his wife would be in hell.

"That's what you get for loving a woman too much," Sexton allegedly told the officers. "Let that be a lesson to both of you."

But during his 1969 trial, Sexton said he couldn't remember what happened that night in 1965. He did say, however, that the first "three or four" years of their marriage had been happy. When they married in Tennessee, he was nineteen and she was sixteen.

Chiappetta, in effect, put the dead woman on trial, arguing that Sexton was driven to murder by his wife, whom he maintained was unfaithful to him and had abandoned their six children. Prosecutors argued that Mildred left home because she was regularly beaten by her husband.

The jury of eleven men and one woman in Sexton's 1969 trial deliberated for about three hours before finding Sexton guilty. Judge Cox sentenced him to life at the Indiana State Prison at Michigan City.

That wasn't the last the Delaware County courts saw of Marvin Sexton, however.

Sexton was back in 1973 after a new trial was ordered by the Indiana Supreme Court. Defense attorney Chiappetta successfully argued that his client should have been given access to a copy of a statement he had made to police after his arrest.

Deputy prosecutor Robert Barnet Jr. emphasized the brutality of the crime.

"Sexton came back inside and slashed his wife's throat from behind, so hard her head hung on her shoulders by a mere thread of flesh," Barnet said.

Delaware County deputy prosecutor Robert Barnet Jr. *Courtesy of the Muncie Newspapers Inc.*

A defense psychiatrist in the 1973 trial testified that he believed Sexton was insane the day he killed his wife. Defense attorney Chiappetta argued that Sexton's life had been "destroyed" by eight years of hospitalization and incarceration.

But Barnet told the jury, "Don't misplace your sympathies. Mildred Hazel Sexton was brutally murdered in a Muncie tavern. She should have your sympathy."

And she did. The jury in Marvin Sexton's second trial, nearly eight years after he killed his wife, found him guilty of second-degree murder. He was sentenced to fifteen to twenty-five years in prison.

The notoriety of Mildred Sexton's murder hung over the tavern for years to come. Even in 2015, people posted in Facebook comment threads about her murder, but few had details. One particularly gruesome but untrue urban legend is that Sexton, after decapitating his wife, threw her head into the middle of Walnut Street.

The ownership of the bar changed in the years following the slaying, as did its name. By the early 1970s, the bar was operating as the Oar House, a name meant to suggest "whore house." Complaints followed, and in January 1971, the name of the bar was changed to "She."

"She" didn't last, however. Within a little more than a year, the bar had been renamed Funky Freddie's and featured "go-go" dancers. The bar was still caught in the crosshairs of the law, however; in the fall of 1973, the Alcoholic Beverage Commission cracked down after the club employed two seventeen-year-olds to dance on the bar.

Within a few years, the tavern where Mildred Sexton died was demolished. A vacant lot is all that remains to mark one of the most notorious murder scenes in Muncie in the 1960s.

BIBLIOGRAPHY

CHAPTER 1

Daily Clintonian (Clinton, IN). "One Convicted, One Freed in Muncie Slaying." March 9, 1950.

Donald Franklin Dalton obituary. obitsforlife.com.

"George E. Gratzer." findagrave.com.

Greensburg (IN) Daily News. "Grand Jury Holds Law Enforcement Lax in Muncie." October 19, 1949.

———. "Politicians Blamed in Two Deaths." October 14, 1949.

Kokomo (IN) Tribune. "Defendant in 'Game' Shooting to Take Stand." March 2, 1950.

Muncie Evening Press and *Muncie Star*. "Shootings, Arrests and Trial." Var. issues, October 1949; February–March 1950.

Muncie Evening Press. "Dalton Escape Causes Uproar." May 7, 1964.

———. "Dalton Gets 2 to 31 Years for Cigar Store Murders." October 18, 1950.

———. "Gratzer Freed of Indictments." December 30, 1950.

———. "One Slayer Held, Pal Escapes." October 13, 1949.

———. "Two Indicted; Cleanup Asked." October 18, 1949.

Muncie Star. "Dalton Back of Bars again at Pendleton." June 6, 1954.

———. "One New Deal Slayer in Jail; Pal on Bond." October 12, 1950.

Rushville (IN) Republican. "Man Involved in Muncie Shooting Caught in Texas." October 26, 1949.

State v. Don Dalton. Court file, Muncie Public Library digital archives.

Terre Haute (IN) Star. "Deathbed Evidence Fought by Defense." March 1, 1950.

———. "'Slim Pits' Fill Muncie, Murder Jurymen Told." March 7, 1950.

Terre Haute (IN) Tribune. "Gunmen Kill 2 in Holdup." October 13, 1949.

———. "Killer Claims Self Defense." October 29, 1949.

———. "Mother of Convicted Slayer Seeks Funds." March 14, 1950.

———. "Poker Game Murder Told." March 2, 1950.

CHAPTER 2

Muncie Star. "Funeral." June 20, 1956.

Muncie Star and Muncie Evening Press. "Crimes Blamed on Gypsies." Var. issues, April–August 1952; summer 1961.

———. "Fortune-telling." Var. issues, 1962–65.

CHAPTER 3

"Andy Bodenmiller." Grave records, Beech Grove Cemetery.

"Frederick Horace 'Fred' Oland" and "Michael Betts." findagrave.com.

Indianapolis Star. "Muncie Man Wounded by Two Highwayman." December 20, 1923.

Muncie Daily Herald. "John Petty Returns." April 18, 1899.

———. "A Murder in Whitely." November 15, 1898.

———. "That Whitely Murder." April 13, 1899.

Muncie Morning News. "An Alibi Relied on by Defense in the Oland Murder Case." April 16, 1899.

———. "Blood Stains Were Found about the Oland Premises." April 14, 1899.

———. "Children's Day in the trial of Fred Oland." April 15, 1899.

———. "Denies It." November 18, 1898.

———. "Freddie Oland Placed on Trial for the Murder of Andy Bodenmiller." April 11, 1899.

———. "'I Knew It Would Be that Way,' Said Fred Oland." April 21, 1899.

———. "Indictment." November 27, 1898.

———. "Murder Mystery." November 22, 1898.

———. "Mysterious Was This Whitely Child's Death Monday Night." November 16, 1898.

———. "New Evidence Introduced Yesterday in the Oland Trial." April 13, 1899.

———. "Out of Jail." December 2, 1898.

———. "Small Boy Confessed to the Murder of Baby Bodenmiller." November 17, 1898.

———. "Tells His Story to the Jury." April 19, 1899.

———. "Will Decide Today." November 27, 1898.

State v. Fred Oland. Court file, Muncie Public Library digital archives.

CHAPTER 4

"Amos Rusie." baseball.reference.com.

"Amos Rusie." findagrave.com.

Arkansas City (KS) Daily Traveler. "Has Been Buried Alive." May 1, 1902.

Boston (MA) Post. "Passing of Amos Rusie." December 8, 1901.

Chicago (IL) Inter-Ocean. "Amos Rusie Drunk in Court." May 5, 1900.

Davenport (IA) Weekly Leader. "Amos Rusie as a Villager." November 30, 1900.

Decatur (IL) Review. "Beno Is Dead." December 30, 1899.

Eau Claire (WI) Leader. "Amos Rusie." June 19, 1910.

Hagerstown (IN) Exponent. "Beno the Freak." August 17, 1898.

———. "Broken Awl Points." January 12, 1898.

Indiana marriages, 1811–2007. familysearch.org.

Indianapolis (IN) News. "Rusie to Remarry." August 7, 1900.

Indianapolis (IN) Star. "Amos Rusie a Life Saver." June 12, 1906.

Louisville (KY) Courier-Journal. "The New Rule of Amos Rusie." December 8, 1901.

Marion (OH) Star. "Man with Sponge Head Passes Away." November 14, 1903.

Minneapolis (MN) Journal. "The Nonpareil Man." November 18, 1903.

Muncie Daily Times. "The Rusie Divorce." May 5, 1900.

Muncie Morning News. "Beno Will Bet." July 7, 1898.

———. "From the Grave." July 6, 1898.

Muncie Morning Star. "Amos Rusie Is in Old Time Form." March 29, 1902.

———. "Amos Rusie Will Umpire." August 19, 1900.

———. "Cincinnati Gets Rusie." December 15, 1900.

———. "Rusie's Wife Files Suit." April 19, 1900.

———. "Rusie Will Pitch Again." September 3, 1900.

Muncie Times. "Beno the Muncie Freak." March 15, 1900.

Pittsburgh (PA) Post. "Divorce for Mrs. Rusie." May 5, 1900.

Reading (PA) Times. "Cy Young Interview." March 2, 1909.

St. Paul (MN) Globe. "Drove Awl Too Far into His Skull." November 29, 1903.

Topeka (KS) Daily Capital. "Queer Freak Who Doesn't Know Enough to Ache When He Hurts." August 24, 1902.

———. "Talents Not Appreciated." May 7, 1902.

Wilmington (NC) Morning Star. "Amos Rusie Signs." December 4, 1896.

Chapter 5

Fort Wayne (IN) Journal-Gazette. "Tommy Teague Dies at Muncie." December 3, 1923.

Greenfield (IN) Daily Reporter. "Judge Was Disgusted." November 25, 1921.

Indianapolis (IN) News. "Bullet Wound Fatal, Dr. Exene Smith in Jail." June 15, 1921.

Indianapolis (IN) Star. "Admits Holdup in Keith Trial." November 17, 1921.

———. "Denies Shooting Voida." November 22, 1921.

———. "Jurors to Investigate Further into Killing." January 27, 1922.

———. "Jury Indicts Dr. Xene Smith." June 24, 1921.

———. "Smith Testifies in Keith Trial." November 18, 1921.

Logansport (IN) Morning Press. "Dr. Xene Smith Sent to Prison." November 10, 1921.

Logansport (IN) Pharos-Tribune. "Bootleggers Paid Money to Officers." December 8, 1921.

Muncie Evening Press. "Brother Tells His Version of Voida Shooting." June 11, 1921.

———. "Compromise Agreed to by Accused." November 9, 1921.

———. "Glen Zoll obituary." February 19, 1973.

———. "Joe Voida Identifies Smith." November 17, 1921.

———. "Jury Ignores Instructions, Acquits Keith." November 24, 1921.

———. "Romanian Shot by Unknown Man at Early Hour." June 10, 1921.

———. "Says Keith Ignorant of Holdup Plan." November 20, 1921.

Muncie Morning Star. "Keith Acquitted of Killing Voida; Jury Denounced." November 24, 1921.

Muncie Star. "Says Glen Zoll Was Fifth Man in Murder Plot." November 10, 1921.

Union City (IN) Times-Gazette. "Union City Man Dies Suddenly; Heart Victim." March 23, 1942.

CHAPTER 6

Edinburg (IN) Daily Courier. "Holland Triplets." May 18, 1935.
Muncie Evening Press. "June Holland Committed." November 26, 1981.
———. "June Holland Held on Murder Charge." March 2, 1981.
Muncie Star and *Muncie Evening Press.* "Triplets." Var. issues, 1951, 1954, 1956, 1972.
Muncie Star. "June Holland Found Not Responsible Because Insane." November 19, 1981.
———. "June Holland Ruled Competent to Stand Trial." May 19, 1981.
———. "Whatever Happened to Holland Triplets?" October 20, 1994.
Pittsburgh (PA) Courier. "Holland Triplets." May 25, 1935.

CHAPTER 7

Muncie Evening Press. "Death." May 27, 1954.
Muncie Post-Democrat. "Gambling." November 9, 1923.
Muncie Star. "Death." May 28, 1954.
Obituary. May 29, 1954.

CHAPTER 8

"Benjamin Harrison Smith." findagrave.com.
"Charles V. Smith." findagrave.com.
Muncie Evening Press, November 2, 1911.
———. "Benadum Says M'Galliard Did Not Kill Girl." January 17, 1912.
———. "Boy Beats His Father to Death with Brick, Hides Body in Well." November 18, 1910.
———. "Defense Planned for Youthful Murderer." November 1, 1911.
———. "Grand Jury Is Called to Indict Smith." November 23, 1910.
———. "'Mental Epilepsy' Is Blamed for Tragedy." January 20, 1912.
———. "M'Galliard on Stand in His Own Defense." January 18, 1912.
———. "Muncie Youth in the State Penitentiary Takes His Own Life." February 6, 1911.
———. "Murder and Dance Cause Chilton Row." November 20, 1911.
———. "Patricide Is Sentenced for Life to Prison." December 1, 1910.
———. "Pleads Guilty to Murder in First Degree." November 30, 1910.
———. "Public Dance Is Prohibited by Police." November 6, 1911.
———. "Youth Hears Fate without Outward Sign." January 22, 1912.

Muncie Morning Star. "Brick Slayer Shows No Trace of Regret." November 19, 1910.

———. "Indication That Murder of Young Girl Was Premeditated." November 2, 1911.

———. "Mother's Sobs Break Courtroom's Quiet." January 18, 1912.

———. "Murder Motive Son's Marriage." November 21, 1910.

———. "Prosecutor Asks for Death Penalty." December 2, 1910.

———. "Young Girl Murdered in Halloween Dance." November 1, 1911.

State v. Benjamin Smith. Court file, Muncie Public Library digital archives.

State v. Charles McGalliard. Court file, Muncie Public Library digital archives.

Chapter 9

Muncie Evening Press. "Helen Nokes Murdered." March 18, 1961.

———. "Suspect's Kin Held in Alleged Threat." June 25, 1961.

Muncie Star and Muncie Evening Press. "First Trial." Var. issues, April 1962.

———. "Fred Cooper Dies in Fire." June 1, 1995.

———. "Investigation, Lie Detectors, Legal Filings." Var. issues, March 1961–January 1962

———. "Murder Charges Filed." April 9 and 10, 1961.

———. "Pre-trial Filings." Var. issues, early 1962.

———. "Second Trial and Pre-trial Motions and Hearings." Var. issues, 1963–64.

Muncie Star. "Charges Dropped against Fred Cooper." May 23, 1968.

———. "Charges Dropped against Raymond Taylor." June 25, 1968.

Chapter 10

Muncie Evening Press. "85-year-old Woman Arrested." January 26, 1972.

———. "Muncie Prostitution History." February 15, 1989.

———. "Primary Election Results." May 8, 1974.

Muncie Star and Muncie Evening Press. "Police Raids, Efforts to Close Babe's." Var. issues, 1967, 1968, 1971, 1972.

———. "Raids on Sebab's Truck Stop." Var. issues, June and July 1973.

Muncie Star. "Babe Swartz Enters Sheriff's Race." March 13, 1974.

———. "Former Babe's Truck Stop Burns." March 18, 1975.

———. "Raid on Babe's Truck Stop." November 16, 1967.

CHAPTER 11

Indianapolis (IN) News. "Muncie Banker Is Killed by Assassin." September 23, 1910.

———. "Muncie's Mystery Still Dark Secret." March 28, 1911.

Leavenworth (KS) Post. "Horse Trails Slayer." September 24, 1910.

Monroe (LA) News-Star. "Woman Involved." April 6, 1911.

Muncie Evening Press. "Black Murder Not Cleared in Its Report." December 28, 1910.

———. "Black Murder Taken Up by Grand Jury." December 20, 1910.

———. "Coroner's Inquest Avails but Little." October 5, 1910.

———. "Murder Mystery Baffles the Police." September 23, 1910.

———. "No Reward Was Offered for Murderer." September 27, 1910.

———. "Who Killed Norman Black?" April 6, 1911.

———. "Why Has Murderer Never Been Detected?" April 7, 1911.

———. "Williamson Arrested by Sheriff." January 6, 1911

———. "Woman in White Is Wanted." September 24, 1910.

Muncie Morning Star. "Did a Woman or a Man Kill Black?" December 2, 1910.

———. "Murder of Norman Black Unavenged." September 22, 1911.

———. "Norman Black Victim of Murderer's Bullet." September 23, 1910.

———. "Red Tape Helps Black's Assassin." September 27, 1910.

———. "Reward Offer Is Now Likely." September 26, 1910.

Pittsburgh (PA) Daily Post. "Supposed Suicide Proves to Be Murder." September 24, 1910.

Rushville (IN) Daily Republican. "Woman Is to Be Questioned." September 30, 1910.

Topeka (KS) Daily Capital. "Wisdom of Old Horse May Revenge Murder." September 24, 1910.

Washington (D.C.) Post. "Banker Slain in Buggy." September 24, 1910.

CHAPTER 12

Muncie Evening Press. "Charges Dismissed." October 22, 1971.

———. "Gambling Machines Seized at Shrine Club." May 2, 1973.

Muncie Star and Muncie Evening Press. "Gambling Crackdown on Slot Machines." Var. issues, April 1971– .

———. "Pinball Crackdowns." Var. issues, 1964.

Muncie Star. "Cigar Store Gambling Raids." October 9, 15, 1971.

———. "Gambling Charges Dismissed." March 1972.

———. "Judge Holds Court in Cigar Store." February 5, 1972.

———. "Man Can Get Gambling Machines Back if Donates $2,000 to Children's Home." October 16, 1982.

———. "Man Charged for Allowing Minor to Pay to Operate World Series Pinball Machine." October 16, 1964.

———. "Sliding Wall Found in Raid at VW Post." April 24, 1971.

CHAPTER 13

"Loyed C. Key" and "Ethel Grace Key." findagrave.com.

Muncie Evening Press. "Court Orders Key Held in Death Probe." March 29, 1965.

———. "First Degree Murder Is Charged by Jury." April 2, 1965.

———. "Key Gets Life Term on Plea of Murder." April 21, 1965.

———. "Key Is Questioned in Wife's Slaying." March 27, 1965.

———. "Mrs. Hazelbaker Guilty in Slaying Case." November 16, 1965.

———. "Slain Woman to Be Buried in Alabama." March 22, 1965.

———. "Woman Fire Fatal Shots, Key Now Says." March 30, 1965.

Muncie Star. "Alexandria Divorcee Denies Mrs. Key's Slaying." April 15, 1965.

———. "Ex-Muncie Resident Shot in Head Six Times." March 22, 1965.

———. "Girlfriend's Statement Links Key to Wife's Death on I-69." March 27, 1965.

———. "Key Again Changes Story of How Wife Met Death." March 31, 1965.

———. "Key Says Didn't Do It after Guilty Plea to Cox." April 22, 1965.

———. "Lie Test for Victim's Husband Set Thursday." March 23, 1965.

———. "Mrs. Hazelbaker Denies Any Role in Slaying of Mrs. Key." November 13, 1965.

———. "Mrs. Hazelbaker Denies Key Version of Slaying." April 1, 1965.

———. "Murdered Woman's Purse Found along Interstate 69." March 25, 1965.

———. "Statements on Key Murder Constantly Changing." April 4, 1965.

Pruitt v. Key. Supreme Court of Alabama ruling.

CHAPTER 14

Muncie Evening Press. "Schlegel Convicted." February 14, 1957.

———. "Schlegel Indicted on Three Counts, Including Second-Degree Murder." August 17, 1956.

———. "Schlegel Trial." Var. issues, January–February 1957.

Muncie Star. "First Word of Missing Couple." April 28, 1956; April 29, 1956.

———. "Funeral for Spade Couple." May 6, 1956.

———. "Investigation Continues." Var. issues, May 1956.

———. "Missing Couple Murdered, Bodies in Gravel Pit, Brother Arrested." May 3, 1956.

———. "Schlegel Gets Life in Prison." February 19, 1957.

———. "Slain Couple's Property Sold at Auction." July 25, 1956.

Chapter 15

Altoona (PA) Tribune. "Life Imprisonment Given Charles 'One Arm' Wolf." November 20, 1925.

Brainerd (MN) Daily Dispatch. "Dutch Anderson Reported Slain." November 2, 1925.

Bridgeport (CT) Telegram. "Wolf, Chapman Gang Member, Found Guilty of Murdering Hances." November 19, 1925.

Columbus (IN) Republic. "Man Named in Hance Slaying Denies Crime." February 17, 1926.

Decatur (IL) Herald. "Million-dollar Bandit' Taken." January 19, 1925.

Edinburgh (IN) Daily Courier. "One-Arm Wolf Freed from Life Sentence." December 14, 1953.

Elwood (IN) Call-Leader. "Lawyers Clash in Wolf Trial." November 18, 1925.

Garrett (IN) Clipper. "Hartford City Woman Is Killed by Her Husband." April 4, 1921.

Indianapolis (IN) News. "Hance Marked Man, Knew It from Time He Turned Informer." August 15, 1925.

Lakeland (FL) Ledger. "Blast Victim Was Ex-Mobster." June 26, 1959.

———. "Ex-Chapman Gang Member Dies Penniless." June 28, 1959.

Muncie Evening Press and Muncie Star. "Chapman Arrest, Hance Slayings, Wolf Trial." Var. issues, January 1925, August 1925, November 1925.

New Philadelphia (OH) Daily Times. "Bravado Unbroken as Sentence Is Passed." April 4, 1925.

———. "Chapman's Betrayer Is Shot by Gangsters." August 15, 1925.

Oneonta (NY) Star. "Chapman Walks with Full Strength to Noose." April 6, 1926.

Scranton (PA) Republican. "Chapman Captured in Indiana after Pistol Battle." January 19, 1925.

State v. Ben Hance. Court file, Muncie Public library digital archives.

State v. Charles Wolf. Multiple files, Muncie Public Library digital archives.

Valparaiso (IN) Vidette-Messenger. "Freedom for Lifer Sought by Brother." March 26, 1935.

Wolf v. State. Indiana Supreme Court decision.

CHAPTER 16

Ball State Daily. "Elliott Hall Haunted." October 4, 2015.

———. "Muncie Civic Theatre." October 4, 2015.

"Beech Grove Cemetery." beechgrovecemetery.com.

Beech Grove Cemetery. Booklet, 1906.

"Beech Grove Cemetery." Handout, n.d.

Disher, John. "Rivoli Theatre." rivolitheatre.wordpress.com.

"Elliott Hall." iweb.bus.edu.

Muncie Star. "Milo Snell obituary." August 29, 1980.

Roberts Hotel, Muncie's Historic Treasure. Booklet, 1987.

CHAPTER 17

Alexandria (IN) Times-Tribune. "Sister Pleads for Her Brother." December 8, 1920.

Fort Wayne (IN) Sentinel. "Conductor Killed in Quarrel over Ten Cents." August 6, 1909.

Hammond (IN) Times. "Clemency Is Again Denies Nelson Ross, Muncie Lifer." October 5, 1937.

Indianapolis (IN) News. "Muncie Sheriff Seizes Witness in Ross Case." October 23, 1909.

———. "A Registered Letter Goes Wrong." April 7, 1900.

Indianapolis (IN) Star. "'Lifer' Wrote Poem Praying for Liberty." November 7, 1914.

Muncie Daily Times. "Nelson Ross Arrested." April 6, 1900.

Muncie Evening Press. "Dr. Nelson Ross Shot and Killed Daniel Linder." August 6, 1909.

———. "Fiancée Died Few Moments after Dr. Ross Had Left Her." August 23, 1908.

———. "Life Behind the Bars for Dr. Nelson Ross." October 26, 1909.

———. "Ross on Stand, Weeps." October 21, 1909.

———. "Ross Was Brave Through Ordeal of Punishment." October 30, 1909.

———. "The Song of Ross Awoke Prisoners." October 22, 1909.

Muncie Morning Star. "Local Physician Will Defy Board." February 20, 1906.

Muncie Times. "Serious Charge Against Ross." December 27, 1902.

State v. Nelson Ross. Multiple files, Muncie Public Library digital archives.

Chapter 18

Muncie Evening Press. "Murder of Willie Oscar Price." February 21, 1964.

———. "Three Men in Court for Killing Wives." September 30, 1969.

———. "Underage Go-Go Dancers at Funky Freddie's." October 3, 1973.

Muncie Star and Muncie Evening Press. "Changes to Name of Tavern." Var. issues, January 15, 1971; January 10, 1975.

———. "Prosecution and Trials of Marvin Hollis Sexton." Var. issues, 1965, 1969, 1973.

Muncie Star. "Muncie Police Telling Taverns to Follow the Law." March 20, 1969.

———. "Murder of Mildred Hazel Sexton." July 18, 1965.

———. "Women Allowed to Sit at Bar in Indiana Taverns." July 3, 1969.

About the Authors

Keith Roysdon is a lifelong writer and journalist. He is a reporter at the *Star Press* newspaper in Muncie, Indiana, where he is the paper's watchdog, covering not only the normal functions of government but also, especially, the abnormal—when things go wrong, when money is misspent and when elected officials misbehave.

He began earning a living in the news business when he was still in high school, and his early career included not only general assignment reporting but also entertainment coverage, including movie, book, live music and theater reviews. He began covering government in 1989 and has also covered business and economic news.

Roysdon has won more than two dozen first-place awards in Indiana newspaper contests, among them awards for community service. In addition to many awards for their work together, he and Douglas Walker won the Kent Cooper Award for story of the year in Indiana for their 2010 Cold Case story on Muncie's most notorious unsolved murders. Roysdon is active on social media, with well-followed accounts on Twitter, Facebook and Instagram.

Veteran journalist Douglas Walker has covered the criminal justice system in east-central Indiana for most of the past three decades. For more than a quarter century, he has served in reporting and editing roles for the *Star Press* and its predecessor, the *Muncie Evening Press*.

Walker has received dozens of awards—for writing, investigative reporting and public service—from state, regional and national journalism organizations. Many have been the result of his collaborations with reporter Keith Roysdon, with whom he also cowrites a weekly column on Muncie politics. The Ball State University graduate is an eighth-generation resident of the Muncie area.

Through his reporting, Walker has taken his readers to hundreds of crime scenes, scores of murder trials, two presidential inaugurations and more than thirty election nights and into the death chamber at the Indiana State Prison for an eyewitness account of an exccution.